Securities & Investment Institute Level 3 Certificate in Investment

G000139594

STUDY BOOK
FSA Financial Regulation

Syllabus version 12

In this November 2007 edition

- A **user-friendly format** for easy navigation
- **Exam tips** to put you on the right track
- A **Test your Knowledge** quiz at the end of each chapter
- A full **index**

APPROVED WORKBOOK

LEARNING MEDIA

Published November 2007

ISBN 9780 7517 4296 1

British Library Cataloguing-in-Publication Data
A catalogue record for this book
is available from the British Library

Published by

BPP Learning Media Ltd
BPP House, Aldine Place
London W12 8AA

www.bpp.com/learningmedia

Printed in Great Britain by
WM Print
42-47 Frederick Street
Walsall
W Midlands, WS2 9NE

Your learning materials, published by BPP Learning Media Ltd,
are printed on paper sourced from sustainable, managed
forests.

£50.00

CONTENTS

1

The Regulatory Environment

INTRODUCTION

The current system of regulation for the UK financial services industry was set up with the establishment of the Financial Services Authority (FSA) as the overall regulator in 2001.

The FSA Handbook is the main source for the rules that must be followed. The rule book is continuing to evolve and recent moves from 'rules-based' regulation to 'principles-based' regulation are intended to lead to a reduction in the volume of detailed rules.

The Securities and Investment Institute (SII) is a widely respected professional body within the industry. In this chapter, we cover the SII's Professional Code of Conduct.

CHAPTER CONTENTS

LEARNING OBJECTIVES

The role of the Financial Services Authority (FSA)

- **Know** FSA's statutory objectives

- **Know** that FSA has the power to make rules in respect of authorisation, supervision, enforcement, sanctions and disciplinary action

- **Understand** the Principles for Businesses and the requirement to act honestly, fairly and professionally

- **Understand** FSA's requirement for firms to treat customers fairly

- **Know** the Statements of Principle and Code of Practice for approved persons

- **Know** the Securities and Investment Institute's Code of Conduct

- **Know** the senior management responsibilities: purpose, apportionment of responsibilities, recording the apportionment, systems and controls, compliance

- **Know** the rationale for the FSA moving to more principles-based regulation

- **Know** the sources of information on principles-based regulation

The regulatory infrastructure

- **Know** the regulatory infrastructure generated by the FSMA 2000 and the status and relationship between FSMA 2000, the Treasury, the Office of Fair Trading, the Financial Services Skills Council and the Financial Services Authority and between the FSA and the RIEs, ROIEs, DIEs, RCHs, MTFs and DPBs

- **Know** the relationship between the Financial Services Authority, Financial Ombudsman Service and the Financial Services Compensation Scheme

- **Know** the role of the Financial Services and Markets Tribunal

- **Know** HM Revenue & Customs' responsibility for issuing regulations for ISAs and PEPs

- **Know** the structure, layout and content of the FSA Handbook

1 THE ROLE OF THE FINANCIAL SERVICES AUTHORITY (FSA)

Learning objective | **Know** the FSA's statutory objectives

1.1 Development of the UK regulatory system

1.1.1 Creation of a single regulator

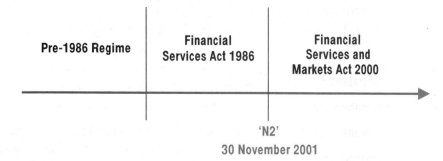

| Pre-1986 Regime | Financial Services Act 1986 | Financial Services and Markets Act 2000 |

'N2'
30 November 2001

Before the advent of the **Financial Services Act 1986**, the UK financial services industry was entirely self-regulating. Standards were maintained by an assurance that those in the financial services industry had a common set of values and were able, and willing, to ostracise those who violated them.

The 1986 Act moved the UK to a system which became known as '**self-regulation within a statutory framework**'. Once **authorised**, firms and individuals would be regulated by self-regulating organisations (SROs), such as IMRO, SFA or PIA. The Financial Services Act 1986 only covered investment activities. Retail banking, general insurance, Lloyd's of London and mortgages were all covered by separate Acts and Codes.

When the Labour Party gained power in 1997, it wanted to make change to the regulation of financial services. The late 1990s saw a more radical reform of the financial services system with the unification of most aspects of financial services regulation under a **single statutory regulator**, the **Financial Services Authority (FSA)**. The process took place in two phases.

1.1.2 Phases of the reforms

First, the Bank of England's responsibility for banking supervision was transferred to the **Financial Services Authority (FSA)** as part of the **Bank of England Act 1998**. Despite losing responsibility for banking supervision, the **Bank of England** ('the Bank') gained the role in 1998 of **setting official UK interest rates**.

The Bank is also responsible for maintaining stability in the financial system by analysing and promoting initiatives to strengthen the financial system. It is also the financial system's '**lender of last resort**', being ready to provide funds in exceptional circumstances.

The **second phase** of reforms consisted of a new Act covering financial services which would repeal the main provisions of the Financial Services Act 1986 and some other legislation. The earlier 'patchwork quilt' of regulation would be swept away and the FSA would regulate investment business, insurance business, banking, building societies, Friendly Societies, mortgages and Lloyd's.

On 30 November 2001, the new Act – the **Financial Services and Markets Act 2000 (FSMA 2000)** – came into force, to create a system of **statutory regulation**. While practitioners and consumers are actively consulted, it is the FSA that co-ordinates the regulation of the industry.

1.1.3 Responding to regulatory failures

The new regime seeks to learn from many of the **regulatory failures** that occurred during the 1980s and 1990s.

- The most widespread problem has been that of **pensions mis-selling**. Salespeople encouraged some 2.2 million people to move out of their employers' schemes into personal pension plans. These transfers were often unsuitable. It is partly this which has led to an increased emphasis in the new regime on educating investors to ensure that they understand the risks of transactions they undertake.

- The Bank of Credit and Commerce International (**BCCI**), an important international bank with many UK offices and customers, was the subject of an £8 billion fraud. This has led to the FSA taking on regulatory responsibility for banks and increased regulation in the field of money laundering.

- The **Barings Bank** crisis was caused by the actions of a single rogue trader, Nick Leeson, whose unauthorised trading, coupled with the inadequacy of controls, led to the collapse of the bank. This has led to a big drive towards ensuring that senior management take their responsibilities seriously and ensure that systems and controls are adequate.

- In a further instance, world copper prices were manipulated by the unauthorised trading of Mr Hamanaka of **Sumitomo**, with much of his trading taking place on the London Metal Exchange. As a result, the new regime introduces more stringent rules to deal with market abuse.

The regulation of the UK financial services industry continues to evolve, and may need to react to new circumstances as they develop.

1.2 FSA as the UK statutory regulator

The creation of the FSA as the UK's **single statutory regulator** for the industry brought together regulation of investment, insurance and banking.

With the implementation of FSMA 2000 at date 'N2' in 2001, the FSA took over responsibility for:

- Prudential supervision of all firms, which involves monitoring the adequacy of their management, financial resources and internal systems and controls, and

- Conduct of business regulations of those firms doing investment business. This involves overseeing firms' dealings with investors to ensure, for example, that information provided is clear and not misleading

Arguably, the FSA's role as **legislator** has been diminished by the requirements of EU Single Market Directives – in particular, the far-reaching **Markets in Financial Instruments Directive (MiFID)**, implemented on 1 November 2007 – as the FSA has increasingly needed to apply rules which have been formulated at the **European level**.

1.3 The FSA's statutory objectives

Section 2 of the Financial Services and Markets Act (FSMA 2000) spells out the purpose of regulation by specifying the FSA's four **statutory objectives**.

The FSA's statutory objectives

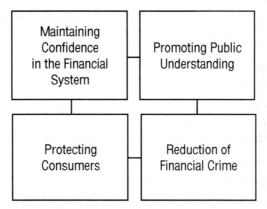

The emphasis placed on these objectives makes FSMA 2000 unusual compared to the Acts that it supersedes – none of which clearly articulated their objectives. FSMA 2000 is seeking to inject much needed clarity into what the regulatory regime is trying to achieve and, perhaps more importantly, seeking to manage expectations regarding what it cannot achieve.

1.4 Status of the FSA

The FSA is not a government agency. Its members, officers and staff are not Crown servants nor civil servants. It is a private company limited by guarantee, with HM Treasury as the guarantor. The FSA is financed by the financial services industry.

The Board of the FSA is appointed by the Treasury and the Chancellor of the Exchequer is ultimately responsible for the regulatory system for financial services under FSMA 2000.

1.5 Functions of the FSA

The FSA's **principal powers** include the following.

- Granting **authorisation** and permission to firms to undertake regulated activities
- **Approving** individuals to perform controlled functions
- The right to issue under **S138 FSMA 2000:**
    - General rules (such as the *Conduct of Business* rules) for authorised firms which appear to be necessary or expedient to protect the interests of consumers
    - Principles (such as the *Principles for Businesses*)
    - Codes of conduct (such as the *Code of Practice for Approved Persons*)
    - Evidential provisions and guidance
- The right to **investigate** authorised firms or approved persons
- The right to take **enforcement** action against authorised firms and approved persons
- The right to **discipline** authorised firms and approved persons

- The power to take action against any person for **market abuse**
- The power to **recognise** investment exchanges and clearing houses
- As the **UK Listing Authority**, approval of companies for stock exchange listings in the UK

Note that the term **'firm'** is used generally in the FSA regulations to apply to an authorised person, whether the person is an individual, a partnership or a corporate body.

2   THE PRINCIPLES FOR BUSINESSES

Learning objective   **Understand** the Principles for Businesses and the requirement to act honestly, fairly and professionally

2.1 Introduction

The **Principles for Businesses (PRIN)** state firms' fundamental obligations under the regulatory system. They are formulated to require honest, fair and professional conduct from firms.

The Principles are drafted by the FSA and derive authority from the FSA's rulemaking powers under FSMA 2000 and from the FSA's **statutory objectives**, and they also include provisions which implement the EU Single Market Directives.

2.2 Application of the Principles

The *Principles for Businesses* apply in whole or in part to every **authorised firm** carrying out a regulated activity. (Approved persons are not covered by these principles, but are instead subject to a separate set of principles, known as **Statements of Principle**, which we shall look at later).

While the *Principles for Businesses* apply to regulated activities generally, with respect to the activities of accepting deposits, general insurance and long-term pure protection policies (i.e. that have no surrender value and are payable upon death), they apply only in a 'prudential context'. This means the FSA will only proceed where the contravention is a serious or persistent violation of a principle that has an impact on confidence in the financial system, the fitness and propriety of the firm or the adequacy of the firm's financial resources.

As we shall see, the implementation of **MiFID** – the EU **Markets in Financial Instruments Directive** – (with effect from **1 November 2007**) has had a significant impact on various aspects of FSA rules. The application of the Principles is modified for firms conducting MiFID business (including investment services and activities, and ancillary services, where relevant), and for EEA firms with the right (often referred to as a '**passport**') to do business in the UK.

2.3 The Principles for Businesses

Listed opposite are the **eleven** *Principles for Businesses*, with a brief description of the activity each relates to.

Principles for Businesses
1. Integrity
A firm must conduct its business with integrity.
2. Skill, care and diligence
A firm must conduct its business with due skill, care and diligence.
3. Management and control
A firm must take reasonable care to organise and control its affairs responsibly and effectively, with adequate risk management systems.
4. Financial prudence
A firm must maintain adequate financial resources.
5. Market conduct
A firm must observe proper standards of market conduct.
6. Customers' interests
A firm must pay due regard to the interests of its customers and treat them fairly.
7. Communications with clients
For customers – A firm must pay due regard to the information needs and communicate information to them in a way that is clear, fair and not misleading.
For eligible counterparties – A firm must communicate information in a way that is not misleading.
8. Conflicts of interest
A firm must manage conflicts of interest fairly, both between itself and its customers and between a customer and another client.
9. Customers: relationships of trust
A firm must take reasonable care to ensure the suitability of its advice and discretionary decisions for any customer who is entitled to rely upon its judgement.
10. Clients' assets
A firm must arrange adequate protection for clients' assets when it is responsible for those assets.
11. Relations with regulators
A firm must deal with its regulators in an open and co-operative way and must disclose to the FSA appropriately anything relating to the firm of which the FSA would reasonably expect notice.

2.4 Scope of the Principles

Some of the principles (such as Principle 10) refer to **clients**, while others (such as Principle 9) refer to **customers**. This difference affects the scope of the relevant principles.

- '**Client**' is an all-encompassing term that includes everyone from the smallest retail customer through to the largest investment firm. It therefore includes, under the terminology of MiFID, eligible counterparties, professional customers and retail customers.

- '**Customer**' is a more restricted term that includes professional and retail clients but excludes 'eligible counterparties'. 'Customers' are thus clients who are not **eligible counterparties**. (We shall see later what is meant by this term.) Principles 6, 8 and 9, and parts of Principle 7, apply only to **customers**.

In line with MiFID, a firm will not be subject to a Principle to the extent that it is contrary to the EU Single Market Directives. Principles 1, 2, 6 and 9 may be disapplied for this reason, in the case of:

- Eligible counterparty business

- Transactions on a regulated market (eg the London Stock Exchange), and member transactions under a **multilateral trading facility** – a system that enables parties (eg retail investors or other investment firms) to buy and sell financial instruments

Note that Principle 3 would not be considered breached if the firm failed to prevent **unforeseeable** risks.

2.5 Breaches of the Principles

The consequence of breaching a Principle makes the firm liable to **enforcement or disciplinary sanctions**. The FSA may bring these sanctions where it can show that the firm has been at fault in some way. The definition of 'fault' will depend upon the Principle referred to.

S150 FSMA 2000 creates a right of action in damages for a '**private person**' who suffers loss as a result of a contravention of certain **rules** by an authorised firm. However, a 'private person' may not sue a firm under S150 FSMA 2000 for the breach of a **Principle**.

2.6 Treating customers fairly (TCF)

Learning objective   **Understand** FSA's requirement for firms to treat customers fairly

In addition to meeting the regulatory objectives, the FSA aims to maintain efficient, orderly and clean markets and help retail customers achieve a fair deal. Since 2000, the FSA has been examining what a fair deal for retail customers actually means. This has led to much discussion of the concept of **TCF** – 'treating customers fairly'.

The FSA does not define **treating customers fairly (TCF)** in a way that applies in all circumstances. By adopting a '**Principles-based approach**' to TCF through Principle 6, the FSA puts the onus on firms to determine what is fair in each particular set of circumstances. Firms therefore need to make their own assessment of what TCF means for them, taking into account the nature of their business.

The FSA wants firms to focus on delivering the following six TCF consumer outcomes.

- Consumers can be confident that they are dealing with firms where the fair treatment of customers is central to the corporate culture.

- Products and services marketed and sold in the retail market are designed to meet the needs of identified consumer groups and are targeted accordingly.

- Consumers are provided with clear information and are kept appropriately informed before, during and after the point of sale.

- Where consumers receive advice, the advice is suitable and takes account of their circumstances.

- Consumers are provided with products that perform as firms have led them to expect, and the associated service is both of an acceptable standard and also as they have been led to expect.

- Consumers do not face unreasonable post-sale barriers imposed by firms to change product, switch provider, submit a claim or make a complaint.

The FSA has set a deadline of end of March 2008 for firms to have appropriate management information or measures in place to test whether they are treating their customers fairly.

2.7 The client's best interests rule

The **Conduct of Business Rules** require that firms must act honestly, fairly and professionally in accordance with the **best interests of the client**. This rule applies to designated investment business for a retail client or, in relation to MiFID business, for any other client.

In communications relating to designated investment business, a firm must not seek to exclude or restrict any duty or liability it may have under the regulatory system. If the client is a retail client, any other exclusion or restriction of duties or liabilities must meet the 'clients' best interests rule' test above. (The general law, including **Unfair Terms Regulations**, also limits a firm's scope for excluding or restricting duties or liabilities to a consumer.)

3 STATEMENTS OF PRINCIPLE AND CODE OF PRACTICE FOR APPROVED PERSONS

Learning objective **Know** the Statements of Principle and Code of Practice for Approved Persons

3.1 Approved persons

Section 59 FSMA 2000 states that a person (an individual) cannot carry out certain **controlled functions** unless that individual has been approved by the FSA. This requirement gives rise to the term '**approved person**', and the FSA's Supervision Manual (SUP) covers the approval process. We look further at the approval process later in this Study Book.

3.2 Statements of Principle for Approved Persons

FSA *Statements of Principle* apply generally to all **approved persons** (i.e. relevant employees of FSA firms) when they are performing a **controlled function**. The scope of 'controlled' functions is covered later in this Study Book.

The Statements of Principle will not apply where it would be contrary to the UK's obligations under EU Single Market Directives. Under **MiFID** rules, the requirement to employ personnel with the necessary knowledge, skills and expertise is reserved to the firm's **Home State**. As a result, the FSA does not have a role in assessing individuals' competence and capability in performing a controlled function in relation to an **incoming EEA firm** providing MiFID investment services.

There are **seven Statements of Principle**. The first four Principles apply to all approved persons (which includes those doing a **significant influence function** as well as those not doing a significant influence function). As noted in the Table below, the final three Principles only apply to approved persons performing a significant influence function.

Statements of Principle for Approved Persons	
1 Integrity	
2 Skill, care and diligence	Apply to all approved persons
3 Proper standard of market conduct	
4 Deal with the regulator in an open way	
5 Proper organisation of business	
6 Skill, care and diligence in management	Apply only to those doing a significant influence function
7 Comply with regulatory requirements	

We now look at the **seven *Statements of Principle*** in detail taking into account the treatment of each by the *Code*.

Statement of Principle 1

> An approved person must act with integrity in carrying out his controlled functions.

The *Code* provides examples of behaviour that would not comply with this Statement of Principle. These include an approved person:

- **Deliberately misleading clients**, his firm or the FSA, or
- Deliberately failing to inform a customer, his firm, or the FSA, that their understanding of a material issue is incorrect.

Statement of Principle 2

> An approved person must act with due skill, care and diligence in carrying out his controlled function.

Examples of non-compliant behaviour under Statement of Principle 2 include failing to inform a **customer,** or his firm, of material information or failing to control client assets.

The coverage of Statement of Principle 2 is similar to Principle 1. The difference is that Principle 1 states that each act needs to be **deliberate**. Principle 2 may be breached by acts which, whilst not deliberate wrongdoing, are **negligent**.

Statement of Principle 3

> An approved person must observe proper standards of market conduct in carrying out his controlled function.

Examples of non-compliant behaviour under Statement of Principle 3 include:

- A breach of market codes and exchange rules
- A breach of the *Code of Market Conduct*

The FSA expects all approved persons to meet proper standards, whether they are participating in organised markets such as exchanges, or trading in less formal over-the-counter markets.

Statement of Principle 4

> An approved person must deal with the FSA and with other regulators in an open and co-operative way and must disclose appropriately any information of which the FSA would reasonably expect notice.

This Statement of Principle concerns the requirement to co-operate, not only with the FSA, but also with other bodies such as an overseas regulator or an exchange.

Approved persons do not have a duty to report concerns directly to the FSA unless they are responsible for such reports. The obligation on most approved persons is to report concerns of '**material significance**' in accordance with the firm's **internal procedures**. If no such procedures exist, the report should be made direct to the FSA.

It would also be a breach of this Statement of Principle if an approved person did not attend an interview or meeting with the FSA, answer questions or produce documents when requested to do so and within the time limit specified.

Statement of Principle 5

> An approved person performing a significant influence function must take reasonable steps to ensure that the business of the firm for which he is responsible in his controlled function is organised so that it can be controlled effectively.

As stated above, Principles 5 to 7 relate only to those approved persons performing a significant influence function. This principle requires those performing a significant influence function to **delegate** responsibilities responsibly and effectively. Paramount to this is a requirement that they should delegate only where it is to a suitable person. In addition, they must provide those persons with proper reporting lines, authorisation levels and job descriptions. Clearly, all of these factors (and in particular the suitability requirement) should be regularly reviewed.

Principle 5 will be particularly relevant to the person whose responsibility it is to ensure appropriate apportionment of responsibilities under the Senior Management Arrangements, Systems and Controls (SYSC) section of the FSA Handbook.

Statement of Principle 6

> An approved person performing a significant influence function must exercise due skill, care and diligence in managing the business of the firm for which he is responsible in his controlled function.

This principle requires those performing a significant influence function to inform themselves about the affairs of the business for which they are responsible. They should not permit transactions or an expansion of the business unless they fully **understand the risks** involved. They must also take care when monitoring highly profitable or unusual transactions and in those or other cases, must never accept implausible or unsatisfactory explanations from subordinates.

This principle links to Principle 5 as it makes it clear that **delegation is not an abdication** of responsibility. Therefore, where delegation has been made, a person must still monitor and control that part of the business and, therefore, should require progress reports and question those reports where appropriate.

Statement of Principle 7

> An approved person performing a significant influence function must take reasonable steps to ensure that the business of the firm for which he is responsible in his controlled function complies with the relevant requirements and standards of the regulatory system.

This has a clear link to Principle 3 of the *Principles for Businesses* – Management and Control. Those exerting a significant influence on the firm must take reasonable steps to ensure that the requirements set out therein are implemented within their firm. They should also review the improvement of such systems and controls, especially where there has been a breach of the regulatory requirements. Principle 7 will be particularly relevant to the person whose responsibility it is to ensure appropriate apportionment of responsibilities under the Senior Management Arrangements, Systems and Controls section of the FSA Handbook.

3.3 The Code of Practice for Approved Persons

FSMA 2000 requires the FSA to issue a code of practice to help approved persons to determine whether or not their conduct complies with the *Statements of Principle*. The FSA has complied with this obligation by issuing the **Code of Practice for Approved Persons (The Code)**. This sets out descriptions of conduct which, in the FSA's opinion, does not comply with any of the statements, and factors which will be taken into account in determining whether or not an approved person's conduct does comply with the *Statements of Principle*. These descriptions have the status of **evidential provisions**.

The Code is not conclusive – it is only evidential towards indicating that a Statement of Principle has been breached. Account will be taken of the context in which the course of conduct was undertaken. In determining whether there has been a breach of Principles 5 to 7, account will be taken of the nature and complexity of the business, the role and responsibilities of the approved person, and the knowledge that the approved person had (or should have had) of the regulatory concerns arising in the business under their control. The examples in the *Code* that would breach a principle are not exhaustive.

In addition, the Code may be amended from time to time and the current published version at the time of the approved person's conduct will be the relevant Code that the FSA will look to in determining whether or not there has been a breach. The FSA will examine all the circumstances of a particular matter and will only determine that there has been a breach where the individual is **'personally culpable'**, i.e. deliberate conduct or conduct below the reasonable standard expected of that person in the circumstances.

4 THE SECURITIES AND INVESTMENT INSTITUTE'S CODE OF CONDUCT

Learning objective	**Know** the Securities and Investment Institute's Code of Conduct

4.1 Introduction

The **Securities and Investment Institute (SII)** is a widely respected professional body for those working in the securities and investment industry.

Familiarise yourself with the SII's Professional Code of Conduct, which is set out below.

4.2 The Professional Code of Conduct

Professionals within the securities and investment industry owe important **duties to their clients**, to the market, the industry and to society at large. Where these duties are set out in law or in regulation, the professional must always comply with the requirements in an open and transparent manner.

Membership of the Securities and Investment Institute **requires** members to meet the standards set out within the Institute's Principles. These principles impose upon members an obligation to act in a way that moves beyond mere compliance and supports the underlying values of the Institute.

A **material breach** of the Principles would be incompatible with continuing membership of the Securities and Investment Institute.

Members who find themselves in a position, which might require them to act in a manner contrary to the Principles, are encouraged to:

1.   Discuss their concerns with their line manager

2.   Seek advice from their internal compliance department

3.   Approach their firm's non-executive directors or audit committee

4.   If unable to resolve their concerns and, having exhausted all internal avenues, to contact the Securities and Investment Institute for advice (email: principles@sii.org.uk)

The Principles	Stakeholder
1. To act honestly and fairly at all times when dealing with clients, customers and counterparties and to be a good steward of their interests, taking into account the nature of the business relationship with each of them, the nature of the service to be provided to them and the individual mandates given by them	Client
2. To act with integrity in fulfilling the responsibilities of your appointment and seek to avoid any acts or omissions or business practices which damage the reputation of your organisation or which are deceitful, oppressive or improper and to promote high standards of conduct throughout your organisation	Firm
3. To observe applicable law, regulations and professional conduct standards when carrying out financial service activities and to interpret and apply them to the best of your ability according to principles rooted in trust, honesty and integrity	Regulator
4. When executing transactions or engaging in any form of market dealings, to observe the standards of market integrity, good practice and conduct required by, or expected of participants in that market	Market participant
5. To manage fairly and effectively and to the best of your ability any relevant conflict of interest, including making any disclosure of its existence where disclosure is required by law or regulation or by your employing organisation	Conflict of interest
6. To obtain and actively maintain a level of professional competence appropriate to your responsibilities and commit to continued learning and the development of others	Self
7. To strive to uphold the highest personal standards including rejecting short-term profits which may jeopardise your reputation and that of your employer, the Institute and the industry	Self

5   SENIOR MANAGEMENT RESPONSIBILITIES

Learning objective   **Know** the senior management responsibilities: purpose, apportionment of responsibilities, recording the apportionment, systems and controls, compliance

5.1 Introduction

The FSA has drafted a large amount of guidance on **PRIN 3** (Principle for Businesses 3). You may recall that this Principle is as follows.

Management and control
A firm must take reasonable care to organise and control its affairs responsibly and effectively, with adequate risk management systems. Note: it would not be a breach of this Principle if the firm failed to prevent unforeseeable risks.

This emphasis comes from a desire to avoid a repetition of the collapse of Barings Bank, where it was clear that management methods and the control environment were deficient.

The FSA suggests that, in order to comply with its obligation to maintain appropriate systems, a firm should carry out a regular review of the above factors.

There is a section of the *FSA Handbook* called '**Senior Management Arrangements, Systems and Controls**'. As the name suggests, the main purpose of this part of the FSA Handbook is to encourage directors and senior managers of authorised firms to take appropriate responsibility for their firm's arrangements and to ensure they know what those obligations are.

Exam tip

The examiner may refer to this Handbook section by its abbreviation as **SYSC**.

5.2 SYSC requirements

A significant requirement of SYSC is the need for the Chief Executive to apportion duties amongst senior management and to monitor their performance. Beyond this, the main issues that a firm is expected to consider in establishing compliance with Principle 3 are as follows.

- Organisation and reporting lines
- Compliance
- Risk assessment
- Suitable employees and agents
- Audit committee
- Remuneration policies

There is a rule regarding apportionment of significant responsibilities, which requires firms to make clear who has particular responsibility and to ensure that the business of the firm can be adequately monitored and controlled by the directors, senior management and the firm's governing body. Details of apportionment and allocation of responsibilities must be recorded and kept up-to-date.

Under non-MiFID rules, record-keeping requirement is for records to be kept for **six years** from the date they are replaced by a more up-to-date record. MiFID requires firms to keep transaction records for **five years**.

Under **SYSC**, the firm has a general obligation to take reasonable care to establish and maintain systems and controls that are appropriate to its business. MiFID firms are required to **monitor and regularly evaluate** the adequacy of its systems, internal control mechanisms and arrangements established to comply with the above. Firms are likely to have to keep additional documentation to meet fully this requirement.

Furthermore, the **compliance function** must be designed for the purpose of complying with regulatory requirements and to counter the risk that the firm may be used to further financial crime.

Depending on the nature, scale and complexity of the business, it may be appropriate for the firm to have a separate compliance function although this is not an absolute requirement. The organisation and responsibilities of the compliance department should be properly recorded and documented and it should be staffed by an **appropriate number of persons** who are sufficiently **independent** to perform their duties objectively. The compliance function should have unfettered access to relevant records and to the governing body of the firm. The MiFID requirements here are broadly in line with the FSA's existing rules.

6 PRINCIPLES-BASED REGULATION

Know the rationale for the FSA moving to more principles-based regulation

Know the sources of information on principles-based regulation

6.1 FSA's approach to regulation

After the establishment of the FSA, there were concerns about the extensive nature of regulation, and the volume of regulatory material which firms were having to follow.

A 'twin approach' was heralded by the FSA, combining 'risk-based' and 'principles-based' aspects.

- The FSA's **risk-based approach** means that it focuses attention on those institutions and activities that are likely to pose the greatest risk to consumers and markets. The FSA considers it both impossible and undesirable to remove all risk from the financial system.

- The 'principles-based' approach implies that, rather than formulate detailed rules to cover the varied circumstances firms are involved in, the Authority would expect firms to carry more responsibility in making their own judgement about how to apply the regulatory Principles and Statements of Principle to their business. The FSA's initiative on **'Treating Customers Fairly' (TCF)** is an example of the Authority's emphasis on principles.

6.2 Implementing principles-based regulation

In its **2006/07 Business Plan**, the FSA signalled its intention to shift, through time, towards more reliance on **higher-level principles**, with fewer detailed rules and thus potentially a slimmer Handbook in future. This focus was re-emphasised in the FSA's **2007/08 Business Plan**, and there has been progress towards reduction in the volume of detailed rules. The incorporation of new **MiFID** rules has helped this process, because the MiFID Directive is generally less wordy and less detailed than the previous FSA rules which have been replaced.

The impact of principles-based regulation has also been seen in **enforcement cases**, where the FSA has relied on its expectation that firms would follow higher-level principles, even where there might not have been breaches of detailed rules. The FSA is deliberately shifting responsibility on to firms to decide what higher level principles mean for them.

6.3 Sources of information

Clearly, **front-line business personnel** should not, in general, be left to interpret higher level regulatory principles in how they carry out their work. The ongoing switch to a principles-based approach means that firms need to develop more of their own **internal rules**. **Senior management** will need to be involved in some of the more important rule-making decisions, which will not generally be left solely to the **compliance function**.

The **Publications section** of the **FSA web site** www.fsa.gov.uk provides a source of various speeches, consultation papers and feedback statements relating to the move towards principles based regulation.

7 THE REGULATORY INFRASTRUCTURE

Learning objective **Know** the regulatory infrastructure generated by the FSMA 2000 and the status and relationship between FSMA 2000, the Treasury, the Office of Fair Trading, the Financial Services Skills Council and the Financial Services Authority, and also the relationship between FSA and the RIEs, ROIEs, DIEs, RCHs, MTFs and DPBs

7.1 The FSA and HM Treasury

As mentioned earlier, the FSA Board is appointed by the **Treasury** and, as the minister with overall responsibility for the Treasury, the Chancellor of the Exchequer is ultimately responsible for the regulatory system for financial services under FSMA 2000.

HM Treasury, to which the FSA is accountable, will judge the FSA against the requirements laid down in FSMA 2000 which includes a requirement to ensure that the burdens imposed on the regulated community are **proportionate** to the benefits it will provide. In delivering against this, the FSA has undertaken a cost/benefit analysis whenever it has increased the burden of a rule.

HM Treasury also requires that the FSA submit an **annual report** covering such matters as the discharge of its functions and the extent to which the four regulatory objectives have been met. HM Treasury also has powers to commission and publish an independent review of the FSA's use of resources and commission official enquiries into serious regulatory failures.

7.2 The Office of Fair Trading (OFT)

7.2.1 The role of the OFT

The **Office of Fair Trading (OFT)** has the goal of helping make markets work well for consumers. Markets work well, the OFT states, 'when fair-dealing businesses are in open and vigorous competition with each other for custom'.

The OFT offers advice, support and guidance to businesses on competition issues and on consumer legislation. It also seeks to promote good practice in business by granting 'approved status' to Consumer Codes of Practice meeting set criteria. The OFT will pursue businesses that rig prices or use unfair terms in contracts.

Under the **Control of Misleading Advertising Regulations**, the OFT works with bodies including the Advertising Standards Authority in exercising its powers to seek injunctions to stop advertising that is deceptive or misleading.

The OFT also regulates the consumer credit market with the aim of ensuring fair dealing by businesses in the market. It operates a **licensing system** through which checks are carried out on consumer credit businesses and it issues guidelines on how the law will be enforced.

7.2.2 The OFT and the FSA

The OFT has specific responsibilities under FSMA 2000.

It is part of the role of the OFT to keep under review the activities and rules of the FSA with respect to competition issues.

If the OFT believes that FSA rules will impact adversely on competition, then it will report this to the FSA, the Treasury and the **Competition Commission (CC)**. The CC is required to report on the matter to the

Treasury, the FSA and the OFT. The Treasury must then decide on any further action, which could include requiring the FSA to change the rules concerned.

7.3 The Financial Services Skills Council (FSSC)

A framework of **appropriate examinations** is being developed by the **Financial Services Skills Council (FSSC)**, which is licensed by the Government. The new **qualifications framework** being developed by the FSSC is the outcome of a wide-ranging Examination Review originally initiated by the FSA.

The **Examination Review** is eventually to cover all qualifications for financial services professionals with the aim of reflecting the needs of the sector in setting up a clear industry-wide, single qualifications framework.

- Standards for appropriate examinations to assess those who will be carrying out particular functions are developed by the FSSC

- Examining bodies (such as the Securities and Investment Institute) can then develop exam schemes in line with the FSSC's standards

The FSA began the Examination Review in 2001 after inheriting as many as 500 approved examination routes and a multitude of designations from previous regulatory bodies. It was considered that this task did not sit comfortably with its role as industry regulator. When the Financial Services Skills Council was formed in 2003, the FSA asked the Financial Services Skills Council to complete the Examination Review and to determine examinations that were appropriate to certain regulated activities.

The Examination Review changed the requirement from **'approved'** exams to **'appropriate'** exams. Under the new 'appropriate exam' regime, lists of appropriate exams covering the common FSSC standards are maintained, although a firm does not necessarily have to choose an exam from this list. It is open to a firm to devise its own 'appropriate examinations' and to present them to the FSSC for endorsement.

7.4 Recognised Investment Exchanges (RIEs)

The act of running an investment exchange is, in itself, a regulated activity (arranging deals in investments) and therefore requires regulatory approval. However, **Recognised Investment Exchange** status exempts an exchange from the requirement. This status assures any parties using the exchange that there are reasonable rules protecting them.

Membership of an RIE does not confer authorisation to conduct regulated activities. Many firms are members of an RIE and also required to be authorised and regulated by the FSA. Membership of an RIE merely gives the member privileges of membership associated with the exchange, such as the ability to use the exchange's systems.

Exchanges with RIE status

- London Stock Exchange (LSE)
- PLUS Markets plc
- LIFFE Administration and Management
- London Metal Exchange (LME)
- ICE Futures
- virt-x Exchange
- EDX London

7.5 Recognised Overseas Investment Exchanges (ROIEs)

As well as the above UK exchanges that are permitted to operate under the RIE status, certain **Recognised Overseas Investment Exchanges (ROIEs)** are permitted to operate in the UK.

Recognised Overseas Investment Exchanges examples:

- NASDAQ
- Chicago Mercantile Exchange (CME)
- New York Mercantile Exchange (NYMEX)
- EUREX

A ROIE is also granted recognition by the FSA.

7.6 Recognised Clearing Houses (RCHs)

This recognition permits the organisation to carry out the clearing and settlement functions for an exchange.

At present there are two **RCHs**:

- Euroclear UK & Ireland Limited (formerly CRESTCo)
- LCH.Clearnet Limited

7.7 Designated Investment Exchanges (DIEs)

In addition to those RIEs in the UK and overseas which the FSA recognises as being effectively run, there are also overseas exchanges that have been given a form of approval yet are unable to conduct regulated activities in the UK.

Designated Investment Exchange (DIE) status assures any UK user of the overseas market that the FSA believes there are appropriate forms of local regulation that guarantee the investor's rights.

The term 'designated' does *not* mean exempt from the requirement to seek authorisation.

Designated Investment Exchanges include, for example:

- Tokyo Stock Exchange
- Toronto Stock Exchange
- New York Futures Exchange
- New York Stock Exchange

7.8 Multilateral Trading Facilities (MTFs)

A **Multilateral Trading Facility (MTF)** is a system that brings together multiple parties (e.g. retail investors, or other investment firms) who want to buy and sell financial instruments, and enables them to do so.

MTFs may be crossing networks or matching engines that are operated by an investment firm or a market operator. Instruments traded on a MTF may include shares, bonds and derivatives.

Changes to FSA rules bring the rules into line with MiFID requirements from 1 November 2007. MiFID requires operators of MTFs to ensure their markets operate on a fair and orderly basis. It aims to ensure this by placing requirements on MTF operators regarding how they organise their markets and the information they give to users.

Additionally, MiFID provides for the operators of MTFs to **passport their services** across borders.

7.9 Designated Professional Bodies (DPBs)

Some of the investment business activities of certain **members of professions**, such as lawyers, accountants and actuaries enjoy an exemption for the requirement for FSA authorisation.

Member firms of '**Designated Professional Bodies**' (**DPBs**) – such as the major accountancy bodies, and the solicitors' Law Society – require **FSA authorisation** if they recommend the purchase of specific investments such as pensions or listed company shares to clients, approve financial promotions or carry out corporate finance business. If the firms' activities are '**non-mainstream**' **investment business**, only assisting clients in making investment decisions as part of other professional services, they are exempt from FSA authorisation but must obtain a **licence** from the DPB, under which they are subject to a lighter form of regulation.

The DPBs are subject to scrutiny by the FSA.

Know the relationship between the Financial Services Authority, Financial Ombudsman Service and the Financial Services Compensation Scheme

7.10 The Financial Ombudsman Service (FOS)

The **Financial Ombudsman Service (FOS)** was set up by Parliament to help settle individual disputes between businesses providing financial services and their customers. The regulations governing complaints are covered in Chapter 6 of this Study Book.

Additionally, the **Consumer Credit Act 2006** has amended FSMA 2000, giving the FOS power to make rules to resolve certain disputes against holders of licences issued by the Office of Fair Trading under the Consumer Credit Act 1974.

FSMA 2000 sets out the roles and responsibilities of the FSA and the FOS. Both organisations are concerned with protecting consumers, but within this overall objective they have distinct and separate responsibilities.

As we have seen, the FSA is responsible for the operation of the regulatory system as a whole, and this includes the establishment and oversight of the FOS.

The FSA's rules require firms to deal with complaints properly. It has power to take disciplinary action against firms and prosecute them under FSMA 2000.

The FOS investigates individual disputes between consumers and regulated firms. Its decision on a dispute can include a monetary award which is binding on the firm (but not on the consumer, unless the award is accepted) of up to £100,000.

7.11 The Financial Services Compensation Scheme (FSCS)

The **Financial Services Compensation Scheme (FSCS)** is designed to compensate **eligible claimants** where a relevant firm is unable or likely to be unable to meet claims against it. Generally speaking, therefore, the scheme will only apply where the firm is declared **insolvent or bankrupt**.

The compensation scheme is independent, but accountable, to the FSA and HM Treasury for its operations and works in partnership with the FSA in delivering the FSA's objectives, particularly that of consumer protection.

FSCS is funded by levies on firms authorised by the FSA. There is more detail on how the FSCS works later in this Study Book.

7.12 The Financial Services and Markets Tribunal

| **Learning objective** | **Know** the role of the Financial Services and Markets Tribunal |

FSMA 2000 makes provision for an independent body accountable to the Ministry of Justice (previously the Department for Constitutional Affairs) (known as the **Financial Services and Markets Tribunal**) which is established under the Financial Services and Markets Tribunal Rules 2001. This provides for a complete rehearing of FSA enforcement and authorisation cases where the firm or individual and the FSA have not been able to agree the outcome. Therefore, if a firm or individual receives a decision notice or supervisory notice or is refused authorisation or approval it may refer this to the Tribunal. The Tribunal will determine what appropriate action the FSA should take and in doing so can consider any new evidence which has come to light since the original decision was made.

7.13 ISA and PEP regulations

| **Learning objective** | **Know** HM Revenue & Customs' responsibility for issuing regulations for ISAs and PEPs |

Some 'wrappers' that can hold UK collective investment schemes, stocks and shares and cash have tax-free advantages. They are **Individual Savings Accounts (ISAs)** and **Personal Equity Plans (PEPs)**. (No new PEPs can be set up, and no new contributions can be made, but existing PEPs can remain open.) These schemes are governed by regulations issued by **HM Revenue & Customs (HMRC)**.

8   THE FSA HANDBOOK

| **Learning objective** | **Know** the structure, layout and contents of the FSA Handbook |

8.1 Primary and secondary legislation

FSMA 2000 – the **primary legislation** – only provides the skeleton of the regulatory system, with much of the detail being provided by **secondary legislation**. Both FSMA 2000 and the secondary legislation are drafted by **HM Treasury**.

Secondary legislation links into various sections of FSMA 2000, fleshing out the requirements and, thus, requiring the two to be read in conjunction. An example of this concerns the authorisation requirement. FSMA 2000 requires that any firm undertaking a **regulated activity** must be authorised or exempt from authorisation. While the routes that a firm may follow to obtain authorisation are contained in FSMA 2000, the meaning of the term 'regulated activity' and the exemptions are found in secondary legislation – namely the Regulated Activities Order.

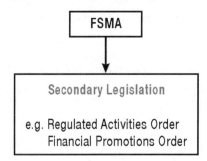

8.2 The role of the FSA Handbook

Earlier we highlighted the link between FSMA 2000 and the secondary legislation. In the day-to-day running of a firm, it will not generally be necessary to pay attention to the legislation and secondary legislation directly. The principles, rules and regulations to which a firm must adhere when running the business are generally found in the **FSA Handbook**. Indeed, even where standards are imposed by FSMA 2000 itself, such as in the case of market abuse and financial promotion, the *FSA Handbook* is used to provide additional requirements.

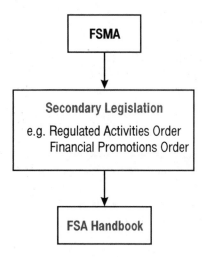

Since 1997, when the move to the new regime was first announced, FSA has undergone a massive consultation exercise. Indeed, hundreds of consultation papers have been released dealing with all aspects of the new regulatory regime. One of the main functions of the consultation process was to alleviate concerns regarding accountability of the FSA and practitioner involvement under FSMA 2000.

The consultation papers resulted in the *FSA Handbook* – a final set of rules, principles and guidance that a firm must adhere to. The FSA derives its power to make rules in the FSA Handbook from FSMA 2000. Therefore, it includes *Principles for Businesses* and various rules contained in the *Conduct of Business Sourcebook*.

Given the range of financial services activities covered, it is hardly surprising that the *FSA Handbook* is a lengthy document. However, as already mentioned, the Handbook is undergoing a process of simplification, in line with the move towards principles-based regulation. This process is partly being carried out in conjunction with the implementation of the Markets in Financial Instruments Directive (MiFID), which has resulted in major changes to the content of the Handbook with effect from 1 November 2007.

8.3 Structure of the FSA Handbook

The *FSA Handbook* is split into seven main blocks.

High Level Standards	Prudential Standards
Principles for Businesses (PRIN)	General Prudential Sourcebook (GENPRU)
Statements of Principle and the Code of Practice for Approved Persons (APER)	Prudential Sourcebooks for Banks, Building Societies and Investment Firms (BIPRU), for Insurers (INSPRU), for UCITS Firms (UPRU) and for Mortgage and Home Finance Firms and Insurance Intermediaries (MIPRU)
Threshold Conditions (COND)	
Senior Management Arrangements, Systems and Controls (SYSC)	
Fit & Proper Test for Approved Persons (FIT)	Interim Prudential Sourcebooks (for Banks, Building Societies, Friendly Societies, Insurers and Investment Business) (IPRU)
General Provisions (GEN)	
Fees Manual (FEES)	

Business Standards
Conduct of Business (COBS)
Insurance: Conduct of Business (ICOB)
Mortgages: Conduct of Business (MCOB)
Client Assets (CASS)
Market Conduct (MAR)
Training & Competence (TC)

Regulatory Processes	Redress
Supervision (SUP)	Dispute Resolution: Complaints (DISP)
Decision Procedure and Penalties Manual (DEPP)	Compensation (COMP)
	Complaints against FSA (COAF)

Specialist Sourcebooks
New Collective Investment Schemes (COLL)
Credit Unions (CRED)
Electronic Money (ELM)
Professional Firms (PROF)
Recognised Investment Exchanges and Recognised Clearing Houses (REC)

Listing Prospectus and Disclosure
Listing Rules (LR)
Prospectus Rules (PR)
Disclosure and Transparency Rules (DTR)

8.4 Handbook guides

Handbook Guides point particular kinds of firm in the direction of material relevant to them in the Handbook. These include guides for Energy Market Participants, Oil Market Participants, Service Companies, Small IFA Firms and Small Mortgage and Insurance Intermediaries.

8.5 Design of the FSA Handbook

The *FSA Handbook* contains a number of different kinds of provisions – including rules, evidential provisions and guidance as follows.

R	This indicates that the corresponding paragraph is a **rule** and means that it places a binding duty on a firm. Most rules are also used to give **private persons** a right of action under **S150**.
E	This indicates that the corresponding paragraph is an **evidential provision**. If a firm complies with an evidential provision, this will tend to establish compliance with the linked rule. If a firm breaches an evidential provision, this will tend to establish that a breach of the linked rule has occurred.
G	This indicates that the corresponding paragraph is **guidance**. Guidance is not binding on a firm but it is used to flesh out particular issues arising from rules.

CHAPTER ROUNDUP

- The Financial Services Authority became the single statutory regulator for the industry in 2001. The Financial Services and Markets Act (FSMA) 2000 provides for a system of statutory regulation of the financial services industry.

- The new regulatory framework was introduced in response to various regulatory failures of the 1980s and 1990s, and replaced an earlier regime of 'self-regulating organisations'.

- Four statutory objectives of the FSA regulatory system are set out in FSMA 2000.

- The FSA has wide powers, including approval of individuals to perform controlled functions, and authorisation of firms. The Authority can issue rules and codes of conduct, can investigate authorised firms or approved persons, and can take discipline and enforcement action.

- The Principles for Businesses (PRIN) state firms' fundamental obligations under the regulatory system, and require honest, fair and professional conduct from firms. The FSA emphasises the principle of Treating Customers Fairly (TCF).

- FSA Statements of Principle apply generally to all approved persons (i.e. relevant employees of FSA firms) when they are performing a controlled function. The Code of Practice for Approved Persons sets out types of conduct breaching the Statements of Principle.

- The Securities and Investment Institute's Code of Conduct includes seven core Principles. If a member encounters a conflict of interest (SII Principle 5), then the member may decide to decline to act.

- The SYSC manual in the FSA Handbook encourages directors and senior managers of authorised firms to take appropriate responsibility for their firm's arrangements and to ensure they know what those obligations are.

- The FSA's 'principles-based' approach to regulation implies that, rather than rely on detailed FSA rules, the Authority expects firms to carry more responsibility in making their own judgement about how to apply regulatory principles to their business.

- The regulatory infrastructure includes the Treasury, the Office of Fair Trading, the Financial Services Skills Council and the Financial Services Authority. Types of institution of which you should have knowledge include RIEs, ROIEs, DIEs, RCHs, MTFs and DPBs.

- The FSA Handbook contains, in a series of blocks, detailed rules which an authorised firm must abide by when conducting business. In addition to Rules, the Handbook contains Evidential Provisions, and Guidance.

TEST YOUR KNOWLEDGE

Check your knowledge of the chapter here, without referring back to the text.

1.	What are the four regulatory/statutory objectives of the FSA?	▪ ▪	▪ ▪
2.	What rights does the FSA have under S138 FSMA 2000?		
3.	List six of the FSA Principles for Businesses.	▪ ▪ ▪ ▪ ▪ ▪	
4.	'S150 FSMA 2000 creates a right of action in damages for a private person who suffers loss from contravention of a rule or principle by an authorised firm.' Is this statement True or False?		
5.	Which Statements of Principle apply to all approved persons?		
6.	Which four parties should an SII member approach if they find themselves in a position which might require them to contravene the SII Principles?	▪ ▪ ▪ ▪	
7.	Who is responsible for developing Appropriate Examinations?		
8.	What is the term applying to a crossing network operated by an investment firm to enable investors to buy and sell financial instruments?		
9.	Give an example of a DPB.		
10.	Can you name the seven blocks of the FSA Handbook?	▪ ▪ ▪ ▪	▪ ▪ ▪

TEST YOUR KNOWLEDGE: ANSWERS

1. Maintaining confidence, promoting public understanding, protecting consumers, reduction of financial crime.

    (See Section 1.3)

2. The right to issue general rules, principles, codes of conduct and guidance.

    (See Section 1.5)

3. You could have listed any six of the following: Integrity, Skill, Care & Diligence, Management and Control, Financial Prudence, Market Conduct, Customers' Interests, Communications with Clients, Conflicts of Interest, Customers: Relationships of Trust, Clients' Assets, Relations with Regulators.

    (See Section 2.3)

4. False. A private person may sue a firm under S150 for the breach of a rule, but not of a Principle.

    (See Section 2.5)

5. The first four Statements of Principle apply to all approved persons. These are: Integrity; Skill, care and diligence; Proper standards of market conduct; Deal with the regulator in an open way.

    (See Section 3.2)

6. (1) Line manager; (2) Internal compliance department; (3) Firm's non-executive directors or audit committee; (4) the SII.

    (See Section 4.2)

7. The Financial Services Skills Council (FSSC).

    (See Section 7.3)

8. Multilateral Trading Facility (MTF).

    (See Section 7.8)

9. Examples include: The Law Society; the Institute of Chartered Accountants in England and Wales.

    (See Section 7.9)

10. The seven blocks of the FSA Handbook are: High Level Standards, Prudential Standards, Business Standards, Regulatory Processes, Redress, Specialist Sourcebooks and Listing, Prospectus and Disclosure.

    (See Section 5.2)

2

The Financial Services and Markets Act 2000

INTRODUCTION

The FSMA 2000 establishes the statutory role of the Financial Services Authority. In this chapter, we look at the range of investments which are covered by the Act, and at the range of activities which are regulated by the FSA under the legislation.

We explain more fully the FSA's enforcement powers which were referred to in the previous chapter. The FSA has wide powers to require information from firms.

Individuals carrying out 'controlled functions' are subject to the 'approved persons' regime, which is a distinct from the process of authorisation of the firms in which such individuals work.

CHAPTER CONTENTS

LEARNING OBJECTIVES

Regulated and prohibited activities

■ **Know** the regulated and prohibited activities

- – Authorised persons
- – Exempt persons and FSMA Exemption Order 2001
- – Offences under the Act
- – Enforceability of agreements entered into with an unauthorised business
- – Penalties for carrying out unauthorised business
- – Defences available under the Act

Performance of regulated activities

■ **Know** the role, scope and consequences of the Regulatory Decisions Committee's responsibility for decision-making and the introduction to the FSA's enforcement division and the power of the FSA to make decisions by executive procedures

■ **Know** the outcomes of the FSA's statutory notices

■ **Know** the disciplinary processes open to FSA: warning, decision, supervisory and final notices

■ **Know** the circumstances in which each of these notices is issued

■ **Know** the firm's right to refer to the Tribunal

■ **Know** the purpose of FSA's disciplinary measures

- – Private warnings
- – Variation of permission
- – Withdrawal of approval
- – Prohibition of individuals
- – Public censure and statement of misconduct
- – Financial penalties

■ **Know** the FSA's powers to seek redress for consumers

■ **Understand** the FSA's actions in respect of prohibition orders and actions for damages and how private clients can sue for damages when a firm is declared in breach

Information gathering and investigations

■ **Know** the FSA's power to require information

Regulated activities

■ **Know** the activities specified in Part II of the Regulated Activities Order

- – Accepting deposits
- – Issuing electronic money
- – Effecting and carrying out contracts of insurance
- – Dealing in investments as principal or agent
- – Arranging deals in investments and arranging regulated mortgages

- Operating a multilateral trading facility
- Managing investments
- Assisting in the administration and performance of a contract of insurance
- Safeguarding and administering investments
- Sending dematerialised instructions
- Establishing a collective investment scheme (CIS) and stakeholder pension scheme
- Advising on investments and regulated mortgage contracts
- Lloyd's
- Funeral plan contracts
- Entering into and administering a regulated mortgage contract
- Agreeing to carry on most regulated activities

- **Know** the main exclusions from the need for authorisation under the FSMA 2000

  - Dealing as principal
  - Advice in newspapers
  - Trustees, nominees and personal representatives
  - Employee share schemes
  - Overseas persons

- **Know** the investments specified in Part III of the Regulated Activities Order

  - Deposits
  - Electronic money
  - Contracts of insurance
  - Securities
  - Instruments creating or acknowledging indebtedness
  - Government and public securities
  - Instruments giving entitlements to investments
  - Certificates representing securities
  - Units in collective investment schemes
  - Rights under a stakeholder pension scheme
  - Options
  - Futures
  - Contracts for differences
  - Lloyd's syndicate capacity and membership
  - Funeral plan contracts
  - Regulated mortgage contracts
  - Rights to or interests in investments
  - Personal pensions
  - Home finance

- **Know** the authorisation procedures for firms

  - The need for authorisation
  - The threshold conditions for authorisation

- **Know** the supervisory process

  - Purpose of FSA's supervision arrangements
  - Focus on a firm's senior management
  - FSA's risk-based approach to regulation – ARROW II
  - FSA's supervisory tools

- **Know** the approval processes for Approved Persons
    - The application process
    - The criteria for approval as an Approved Person

- **Understand** the FSA's controlled functions: the five functional areas, the main roles within each, the four areas of significant influence functions, the requirement for FSA approval prior to appointment

- **Know** the Training and Competence regime:
    - The application of the systems and control responsibilities in relation to the competence of employees

    - The requirements for Approved Persons

    - The requirements for staff dealing with retail clients

- **Know** the legal and regulatory basis for whistleblowing

Miscellaneous offences under FSMA 2000

- **Know** the purpose, provisions, offences and defences of S397 FSMA 2000 – Misleading Statements and Practices

1 REGULATED AND PROHIBITED ACTIVITIES

earning objective **Know** the regulated and prohibited activities: authorised persons; exempt persons and FSMA Exemption Order 2001; offences under the Act; enforceability of agreements entered into with an unauthorised business; penalties for carrying out unauthorised business; defences available under the Act

1.1 The general prohibition

Section 19 FSMA 2000 contains what is known as the **general prohibition**.

The general prohibition states that no person can carry on a regulated activity in the UK, nor purport to do so, unless they are either **authorised or exempt**.

The definition of person here includes both **companies and individuals**. The list of exemptions and exclusions are set out in the regulations. There is no right to apply for an exemption from S19 if you do not fall into the existing categories.

The sanctions for breaching S19 are fairly severe, namely: criminal sanctions, unenforceability of agreements, compensation, and actions by the FSA to restrain such activity.

1.2 Criminal sanctions and defence

Breach of the general prohibition is an offence punishable in a court of law.

The courts have a lower level, known as a Magistrates' Court, where summary offences are heard, and a higher level with a judge and jury, known as the Crown Court, where indictable offences are heard.

The maximum penalties for conducting unauthorised regulated activities are set out in S23 FSMA 2000:

- **Magistrates' Court:** six months' imprisonment and/or a £5,000 fine
- **Crown Court:** two years' imprisonment and/or an unlimited fine

It is a **defence** for a person to show that all reasonable precautions were taken and all due diligence exercised, to avoid committing the offence.

1.3 Unenforceable agreements

As a consequence of the general prohibition, an agreement made by an **unauthorised** firm will be **unenforceable** against the other party.

FSMA 2000 makes it clear that agreements are not illegal or invalid as a result of a contravention of the general prohibition: they are merely '**voidable**'. This ensures that the innocent party to the agreement may still be able to enforce the agreement against the other party, even though the performance may be a criminal offence.

1.4 Compensation

The innocent party will be entitled to recover **compensation** for any loss sustained if the agreement is made unenforceable.

1.5 Injunctions and restitution orders

The FSA may seek **injunctions** and **restitution orders** to restrain the contravention of the general prohibition and seek to remove the profits from offenders.

1.6 The requirement for authorisation

As stated above, no person can carry on a regulated activity in the UK, nor purport to do so, unless they are either **authorised** or **exempt**.

The **Perimeter Guidance Manual (PERG)** in the FSA Handbook gives guidance about the circumstances in which authorisation is required, or exempt person status is available, including guidance on the activities which are regulated under FSMA 2000 and the exclusions which are available.

The following decision chart indicates the questions to be asked in establishing **whether a firm needs to be authorised**.

Does My Firm Need Authorisation?

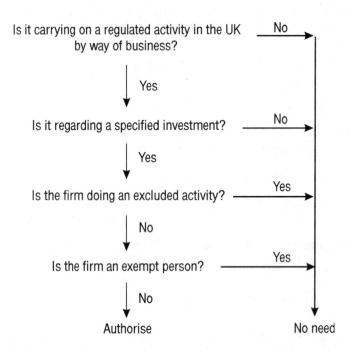

1.7 Exempt persons

The following are the types of person that are **exempt** from the requirement to seek authorisation under FSMA 2000.

- **Appointed representative.** In markets such as life assurance, the bulk of sales takes place through self-employed individuals who act on behalf of the companies. As the companies do not employ them, if this exemption were not in place, such persons would need separate authorisation. The exemption removes them from the scope of authorisation so long as they act solely on behalf of one firm and that firm takes complete responsibility for their actions.
- **Members of professions.** Solicitors, accountants and actuaries have been giving investment advice for many years. As long as giving such advice does not constitute a major proportion of their business (i.e. is incidental) and they are not separately paid for those activities, they are exempt

BPP
LEARNING MEDIA

from the requirement to seek authorisation. However, they will still be governed by their professional bodies (e.g. the Law Society, for solicitors). These professional bodies are known as **Designated Professional Bodies (DPBs)** and are subject to scrutiny by the FSA.

- **Certain persons listed in the Financial Services and Markets Act (Exemption) Order 2001**, including supranational bodies, municipal banks, local authorities, housing associations, the national grid, trade unions, the Treasury Taskforce, the English Tourist Board, government organisations (such as Bank of England, other central banks, an enterprise scheme, the International Monetary Fund and the UK's National Savings & Investments). In addition, charities and the Student Loans Company are exempt in respect of deposit-taking activities. The Financial Services and Markets Act (Exemption) Order 2001 is written by HM Treasury under powers set out in s38 FSMA 2000.

- **Members of Lloyd's**. The requirement to seek authorisation is disapplied for members of Lloyd's writing insurance contracts. The Society of Lloyd's, however, is required to be authorised. This exemption covers **being** a Lloyd's member but does not cover the activities of **advising** on Lloyd's syndicate participation or **managing** underwriting activities.

- **Recognised Investment Exchanges (RIEs), Recognised Overseas Investment Exchanges (ROIEs)** and **Recognised Clearing Houses (RCHs)**.

Exam tip

The word **APRIL** can be used to help learn the five types of exempt persons.

Appointed representatives
Professional people, e.g. solicitors, accountants and actuaries
RIE, ROIEs and RCHs
Institutions who are exempt, e.g. the Bank of England
Lloyd's members

2 PERFORMANCE OF REGULATED ACTIVITIES

2.1 Regulatory Decisions Committee (RDC)

Learning objective

Know the role, scope and consequences of the Regulatory Decisions Committee's responsibility for decision-making and the introduction of FSA's enforcement division and the power of the FSA to make decisions by executive procedures

The FSA's **Enforcement Division** investigates when firms breach FSA rules or the provisions of FSMA 2000. Enforcement staff prepare and recommend action in individual cases. For more significant decisions (called **statutory notice decisions**) the FSA passes the case to another body which is a separate Committee of the FSA, called the **Regulatory Decisions Committee (RDC)**.

The RDC will look at the case and decide whether or not to take action. This would cover the giving of fines, censures, restitution orders, and withdrawing, varying or refusing authorisation or approval. For less serious disciplinary actions, e.g. requesting the firm to provide reports, the FSA may act itself under its '**executive procedures**'.

The RDC is appointed by the FSA Board to exercise certain regulatory powers on its behalf. It is accountable to the board of the FSA for the decisions. However, the RDC is outside the FSA management structure and apart from the Chairman of the RDC, none of the RDC's members are FSA employees. The RDC members comprise practitioners and suitable individuals representing the public interest.

If the RDC decide to take action:

- A **Warning Notice** will be sent, containing details of the proposed action. The person concerned then has access to the material which FSA is relying on and may make **oral or written representations** to the RDC.

- The RDC will then issue a **Decision Notice** detailing the reasons for the decision, proposed sanction and a notice of the right to refer the matter to the Financial Services and Markets Tribunal, which undertakes a complete rehearing of the case.

- When a decision notice is accepted, or appeals finalised, a **final notice** is sent to the person.

A Final Notice only contains FSA/RDC/Tribunal discipline, not any disciplinary action the firm has taken itself internally. The process is summarised in the following table.

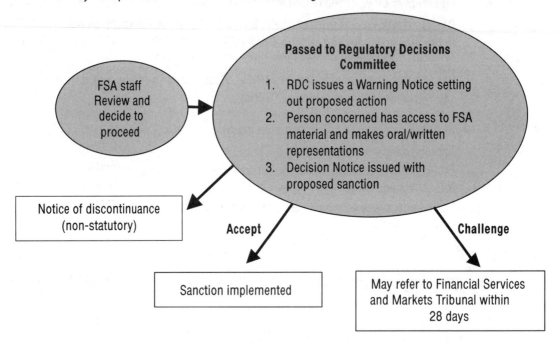

Under Part V of FSMA 2000, the FSA must commence disciplinary action within **two years** of first being aware of the misconduct.

2.2 Disciplinary processes

Learning objectives

Know the outcomes of the FSA's Statutory Notices

Know the disciplinary process open to FSA: warning, decision, supervisory and final notices

Know the circumstances in which each of the notices is issued

Disciplinary measures are one of the regulatory tools available to the FSA. The FSA must be proportionate in its use of disciplinary measures: 'the punishment must fit the crime'. The disciplinary process has been designed to ensure that it is compliant with human rights legislation. Therefore, while FSA staff will investigate the matter and decide whether they feel enforcement action is appropriate, they will not take the final decision on matters of such regulatory significance.

The FSA can take decisions themselves under their own **executive procedures** for matters of lesser regulatory impact to the firms, such as imposing a requirement on a firm to submit regular reports covering activities such a trading, complaints or management accounts. As we have seen, more significant decisions are made by the **RDC** (Regulatory Decisions Committee).

We have also seen that, under FSMA 2000, a variety of notices may be issued. These include Warning Notices, Decision Notices and Supervisory Notices, which are called **statutory notices**. In addition to these Statutory Notices, there are other related notices.

The different types of notice are summarised below.

2.3 Statutory notices

- **Warning notice**: gives the recipient details about action the FSA/RDC proposes to take and the recipient's right to make representations.

- **Decision notice**: gives the recipient details of the action the FSA/RDC has decided to take subject to the RDC going through its formal procedures.

- **Further decision notice**: gives the recipient details of different action the FSA/RDC has decided to take subsequently to giving the original Decision Notice. This can only be given where the recipient consents.

- **Supervisory notice**: gives the recipient details about action the FSA/RDC has taken or proposes to take, normally with immediate effect, i.e. prior to formal procedures. In the FSA's Decision Procedure and Penalties Manual (DEPP), the supervisory notice about a matter first given to the recipient is referred to as the **first supervisory notice** and the supervisory notice given after consideration of any representations is referred to as the **second supervisory notice**.

2.4 Non-statutory notices

- **Notice of discontinuance**: is issued where proceedings set out in a decision or warning notice are being discontinued.

- **Final notice**: sets out the terms of the action the FSA/RDC has decided to take and the date it takes effect from.

2.5 Factors influencing disciplinary action

In determining whether or not to take disciplinary action, the FSA will consider the full circumstances of the case. Some of the factors they may consider are as follows.

- The **nature and seriousness** of the breach, including:
  - Whether the breach was deliberate or reckless
  - Whether the breach reveals serious or systemic weaknesses of the firm's management systems or internal controls of a firm
  - The loss or risk of loss to consumers and market users
- The **conduct** of the firm or approved person after the breach, including:
  - How quickly, effectively, and completely, the firm or approved person brought the breach to the attention of the FSA
  - Any remedial steps the firm or approved person has taken since the breach, e.g. compensating consumers and any internal disciplinary action
- The **previous regulatory record** of the firm

In certain cases, the FSA may determine that it is not appropriate to bring formal disciplinary proceedings, for example, if the conduct is minor or where full remedial action was taken by the firm or approved person themselves (although these facts are not necessarily conclusive that the FSA will not bring formal proceedings).

If the FSA think it would be beneficial for the approved person or firm to know that they were close to being the subject of formal proceedings, then the FSA can issue a **Private Warning**.

- A Private Warning will state that, while the FSA has cause for concern, it does not intend to take formal proceedings.

- A Private Warning will form part of the firm or approved person's compliance history and may be relevant when determining future proceedings.

- The recipient of the Private Warning is asked to acknowledge receipt and may comment on the warning if they wish to.

2.6 Right to refer to the Tribunal

Learning objective	**Know** the firm's right to refer to the Tribunal

FSMA 2000 states that the FSA may not publish information if it would be unfair to the person to whom it relates. The effect of this is that no Warning Notice or Decision Notice may be published by the FSA or the person to whom it is given until reference to the Tribunal has been dealt with and it is clear of further appeals. Therefore, it will be the details of the Final Decision Notice which will be published by the FSA, not the original Decision or Warning Notice.

A person who receives a Decision Notice or Supervisory Notice (including a third party who has been given a copy of the Decision Notice) has the right to refer the decision to the **Financial Services and Markets Tribunal**.

The Tribunal is not bound by earlier proceedings, it can increase or reduce the penalty and can look at new evidence.

2.7 FSA powers and redress for consumers

Learning objectives	**Know** the purpose of the FSA's disciplinary measures: Private warnings; Variation of permission; Withdrawal of approval; Prohibition of individuals; Public censure and statement of misconduct; Financial penalties
	Know the FSA's powers to seek redress for consumers
	Understand the FSA's actions in respect of prohibition orders and actions for damages and how private clients can sue for damages when a firm is declared in breach

The FSA may discipline authorised firms or approved persons for acts of misconduct in order to pursue its regulatory objectives. The detail is contained in the **Enforcement Guide** of the FSA Handbook.

Disciplinary measures against approved persons and authorised firms include the following.

- **Public censure and statements of misconduct**

    The FSA may issue a public censure to a firm where the firm has contravened a requirement imposed under FSMA 2000. The FSA may issue a public statement of misconduct to an approved person where the approved person is guilty of **'misconduct'**. Misconduct means breaching a Statement of

Principle or being knowingly concerned in the contravention of a regulatory requirement by their firm. The FSA will issue a **Warning Notice** of its intention to censure in this way.

In determining whether to issue a censure/statement of misconduct or give a financial penalty the FSA will look at all the relevant circumstances including:

– Whether the accused made a profit or avoided a loss as a result of the misconduct – if so, a financial penalty may be more appropriate

– Whether the accused has admitted the breach, co-operated with the FSA or compensated consumers – if so a censure/statement of misconduct may be more appropriate

– The accused's disciplinary record/compliance history – a poor record or history may make a financial penalty more appropriate

More serious breaches are more likely to receive a financial penalty.

- **Financial penalties, i.e. unlimited fines**

The FSA will impose a financial penalty on a firm where the firm has contravened a requirement imposed under FSMA 2000. The FSA may impose a financial penalty on an approved person where the approved person is guilty of 'misconduct' (as defined earlier). The FSA can also impose a financial penalty on any person who has committed market abuse and also on an applicant for listing or an issuer of listed securities where the UKLA listing rules have been breached. In determining the **size of the penalty** the FSA must have regard to:

– The seriousness of the misconduct
– The extent to which the misconduct was deliberate or reckless
– Whether the person on whom the penalty is to be imposed is an individual

To impose a financial penalty, the FSA must give the individual a **Warning Notice** followed by a **Decision Notice** and a **Final Notice** and the individual must be able to refer the matter to the **Financial Services and Markets Tribunal**. Financial penalties are normally published via a press release unless it would be unfair on the person to whom the penalty is imposed or prejudicial to the interests of consumers.

- **Restitution order/redress**

Where a person (whether authorised or not) has breached a relevant requirement the FSA has powers to require that person to effect restitution on the affected consumers (i.e. **restore them in the pre-breach situation**). In determining whether to exercise its powers, the FSA will have regard to the circumstances of the case and also other facts, including other ways the consumer might get redress and whether it would be more effective or cost effective for the FSA to require redress.

The FSA will also consider any proposals that have already been made. Although this power can be applied for all consumers, the FSA is likely to use the power to provide restitution for market counterparties only in very limited circumstances as they have the resources to fight their own battles.

In order to obtain restitution for a consumer the FSA may need to apply to the court for such an order. The court will make an order for restitution where it is satisfied a requirement has been breached and that the accused has made profits or others have suffered loss or been adversely affected as a result of the breach. The court can then order the accused to pay sums as are just in the circumstances. The awards are often made out to the FSA, who then distribute them to affected consumers.

In addition to the disciplinary measures mentioned above, the FSA can take the following **preventative or remedial action**.

- **Cancellation or variation of authorisation or approval**

  Under FSMA 2000, the FSA may **vary** a Part IV permission where:

  – The firm is failing or likely to fail to meet the threshold conditions for one or more of the regulated activities in respect of which it has Part IV permission

  – The firm has not carried out a regulated activity for which it has a Part IV permission for at least 12 months, or

  – It is desirable to protect consumers

  The FSA will consider **cancelling** a firm's Part IV permission where:

  – It has very serious concerns about a firm or the way its business has been conducted, or

  – The firm's regulated activities have come to an end and it has not applied for its permissions to be cancelled

As we shall see later in the chapter, individuals must be **approved** by the FSA to perform specified **controlled functions**.

Approval may be removed if the individual is no longer fit and proper to conduct that controlled function. To withdraw approval the FSA must give the individual a warning notice followed by a Decision Notice and the individual must be able to refer the matter to the Financial Services and Markets Tribunal.

In deciding whether to withdraw approval, the FSA will take into account the controlled functions being performed and a variety of factors including qualifications and training; the fit and proper criteria (e.g. honesty, integrity, reputation, competence, capability, financial soundness); whether the approved person has breached a statement of principle or been involved in his firm breaching a rule. The FSA will also consider the severity of the risk posed to consumers and confidence in the financial system and look at the individual's disciplinary record. Final notices of withdrawal of approval are normally published unless this would prejudice the interests of consumers.

Furthermore, **S56 FSMA 2000** allows the FSA to prohibit individuals from carrying out specified functions in relation to regulated activities within the investment industry. This is called a **Prohibition Order** and may be issued in respect of anyone whether they are approved or not.

The FSA will exercise its power to make a Prohibition Order where it determines that the individual represents a risk to consumers or confidence in the market generally and is not fit and proper to carry out that function. The order may relate to specified regulated activities or to the activities done by a particular firm or firms. To issue a Prohibition Order it must give the individual a Warning Notice followed by a Decision Notice and the individual must be able to refer the matter to the Financial Services and Markets Tribunal. This process is discussed in more detail later.

A Prohibition Order is much wider than the withdrawal of approval. If the FSA wishes to discipline an approved person, they can use either the withdrawal of approval route or issue a Prohibition Order. However, the FSA will only issue a Prohibition Order if the degree of risk to consumers or confidence in the financial system cannot be addressed by simply withdrawing approval for the relevant controlled function.

In deciding whether to make a Prohibition Order, the FSA will look at the same type of factors as for the withdrawal of approval mentioned above. An unapproved person breaching a Prohibition Order is subject to a **maximum fine of £5,000** (also known as a **level 5 fine**).

Final notices of the issue of Prohibition Orders are normally **published**.

2.8 Rights of private persons

As mentioned in Chapter 1 of this Study Book, **Section 150** FSMA 2000 creates a right of action, in damages, for a '**private person**' who suffers loss as a result of a contravention of certain rules by an authorised firm. A **private person** means individuals not doing a regulated activity, and businesses, in very limited circumstances (where the loss does not arise from their business activities, e.g. setting up an occupational pension scheme for their employees).

This right exists in addition to common law actions, such as negligence or misrepresentation. However, S150 provides a privileged right of action since there is no need to prove negligence. It is sufficient that there has been a **rule breach** leading to **loss**.

Section 59 FSMA 2000 states that a person cannot carry out a **controlled function** in a firm unless that individual has been **approved** by the FSA. We look at the approval process later in this chapter. Note that we are now referring to the individual members of staff of an authorised firm.

If a person is performing a controlled function and is not approved, this is known as a **breach of statutory duty** and a private person has the right to sue their firm for damages if they have suffered loss, using **S71** FSMA 2000, just as they have for a breach of rules under S150.

3 INFORMATION GATHERING AND INVESTIGATIONS

Know the FSA's power to require information

Under **S165** FSMA 2000, the FSA may, by written notice, require an authorised firm (or any person connected with it) or certain other persons (e.g. RIEs) to produce specified information or documents, which it reasonably requires. The FSA can require the information or documents to be provided within a specified, reasonable timescale and at a specified place. The FSA may also require that the information provided is verified and documents are authenticated.

The FSA may require access to an authorised firm's premises on demand: **no notice** need be given.

The FSA may also require a report from a skilled person (e.g. an accountant).

Finally, the FSA may launch an investigation on a number of grounds, including:

- (For an authorised firm) where it has good reason to do so
- Where any person has contravened specific provisions of the regulatory regime (e.g. market abuse)
- At the request of an overseas regulator

While the FSA will normally give the subject of the investigation written notice, it can commence an investigation without doing this if it feels that the provision of the notice may result in the investigation being frustrated.

During the course of an investigation, there is no automatic requirement that the firm or an approved person cease trading.

FSMA 2000 gives sweeping powers to investigators. Generally, the FSA can also require a person under investigation or any connected person to attend at a specified time and place for questioning. The FSA may also require a person to **produce documents** (of which the investigator may take copies only).

Failure to co-operate with an investigator without reasonable excuse is a **criminal offence**. The FSA may also take action themselves such as increasing the severity of the sanction for the original breach. This effectively removes a person's right to silence. In order to ensure that the regime is compliant with human rights legislation, such answers will not be admissible in criminal or market abuse proceedings.

The FSA will not normally make public the fact that it is or is not investigating a particular matter or the outcome of any investigation.

4 REGULATED ACTIVITIES

4.1 List of activities regulated

What range of activities are **regulated activities**? The activities regulated by FSMA 2000 are set out in the **Regulated Activities Order** (as amended).

- **Accepting deposits.** These must be accepted by way of business to be covered.

- **Issuing electronic money.** Some banks and building societies issue 'e-money' which is a form of electronic money that can be used (like notes and coins) to pay for goods and services.

- **Effecting and carrying out contracts of insurance.** After date 'N2' (30 November 2001), the FSA took responsibility for regulating all insurers for capital adequacy purposes and life insurance firms for Conduct of Business Rules. Since January 2005, the FSA has regulated the sales and administration of general insurance as well as life insurance.

- **Dealing in investments as principal or agent.** This covers buying, selling, subscribing or underwriting investments.

- **Arranging deals in investments and arranging regulated mortgages.** This covers making, offering or agreeing to make any arrangements with a view to another person buying, selling, subscribing or underwriting investments. It also covers most mortgages, but generally does not cover buy-to-let or second charge loans. The FSA started to regulate mortgages in October 2004.

- **Operating a multilateral trading facility**. As mentioned in Chapter 1 of this Study Book, this is a system which may be operated by an investment firm that enables parties, who might typically be retail investors or other investment firms, to buy and sell financial instruments.

- **Managing investments.**

- **Assisting in the administration and performance of a contract of insurance** (see above).

- **Safeguarding and administering investments** or arranging such activities.

- **Sending dematerialised instructions.** This relates to the use of computer-based systems for giving instructions for investments to be transferred.

- **Establishing a collective investment scheme or stakeholder pension.** This would include the roles of the trustee and the depository of these schemes.

- **Advising on investments, regulated mortgage contracts, or home finance contracts.**

- **Lloyd's market-related activities.** Lloyd's is the UK's largest insurance market.

- **Providing funeral plan contracts.**

- **Entering into and administering a regulated mortgage contract or home finance contract.** Initially, the FSA regulated mortgage lending only, but since 31 October 2004 the FSA has regulated mortgage advice and administration, in addition to mortgage lending.

- **Agreeing to carry on most regulated activities.** This is itself a regulated activity and so a firm must get the appropriate authorisation before agreeing to do business such as dealing or arranging for clients.

As you can see from the above list, the activities regulated cover the investment industry, banking, insurance and mortgage lending industries, and Lloyd's.

4.2 Activities carried on by way of business

Note that the regulated activity must be carried on '**by way of business**' for the regulations to apply. Whether something is carried on by way of business is, ultimately, a question of judgement: in general terms it will depend on the degree of continuity and profit. HM Treasury has also (via secondary legislation) made explicit provisions for certain activities, such as accepting deposits. This will not be regarded as carried on by way of business if a person does not hold himself out as doing so on a day-to-day basis, i.e. he only accepts deposits on particular occasions. An example of this would be a car salesman accepting a down payment on the purchase of a car.

4.3 Excluded activities

earning objective | **Know** the main exclusions from the need for authorisation under the FSMA 2000

As set out in PERG, the following activities are **excluded** from the requirement for authorisation.

- **Dealing as principal where the person is not holding themselves out to the market as willing to deal.** The requirement to seek authorisation does not apply to the personal dealings of unauthorised individuals for their own account, i.e. as customers of an authorised firm. It would also exclude companies issuing their own shares.

- **Trustees, nominees and personal representatives.** These persons, so long as they do not hold themselves out to the general public as providing the service and are not separately remunerated for the regulated activity, are excluded from the requirement to seek authorisation.

- **Employee share schemes.** This exclusion applies to activities which further an employee share scheme.

- **Media**, e.g. TV, radio and newspapers. Many newspapers and other media give investment advice. However, provided this is not the primary purpose of the newspaper, then under the exceptions granted within FSMA 2000, it need not seek formal authorisation. On the other hand, the publication of '**tip sheets**' (written recommendations of investments) will require authorisation.

- **Overseas persons.** Overseas persons are firms which do not carry on regulated activity from a permanent place within the UK. This exception covers two broad categories: first, where the activity requires the direct involvement of an authorised or exempt firm and, second, where the activity is carried on as a result of an unsolicited approach by a UK individual. Thus, if a UK individual asks a fund manager in Tokyo to buy a portfolio of Asian equities for them, the Japanese firm does not need to be authorised under FSMA 2000.

Exam tip

> Use the word **DEMOTE** to help you to learn the five excluded activities.
>
> **D**ealing as principal, where the person is not holding themselves out to the market as willing to deal
> **E**mployee share schemes
> **M**edia
> **O**verseas persons
> **T**rustees
> Nomin**E**es and personal representatives

4.4 Specified investments

earning objective | **Know** the investments specified in Part III of the Regulated Activities Order

Only activities relating to **specified investments** are covered by FSMA 2000. Specified investments are also defined in the **Regulated Activities Order** (as amended). In general terms, these are as follows.

■ **Deposits.** Simply defined, this is a sum of money paid by one person to another under the terms that it will be repaid on a specified event (e.g. on demand).

■ **Electronic money.** This is defined as monetary value, as represented by a claim on the issuer, which is stored on an electronic device, is issued on receipt of funds and is accepted as a means of payment by persons other than the issuer.

■ **Contracts of insurance.** Included in this category are general insurance contracts (such as motor insurance, accident or sickness), long-term insurance contracts (such as life and annuity) and other insurance contracts (such as funeral expense contracts).

■ **Shares** or stock in the capital of a company wherever the company is based.

■ **Debentures, loan stock and similar instruments**, e.g. certificate of deposit, Treasury bills of exchange, floating rate notes, bulldog bonds and unsecured loan stock (but not cheques or other bill of exchange, banker's drafts, letters of credit, trade bills or Premium Bonds).

■ **Government and public securities**, e.g. gilts, US Treasury bonds (not National Savings & Investments products, such as Premium Bonds and National Savings Certificates).

■ **Warrants.** A warrant gives the right to buy a new share in a company.

■ **Certificates representing certain securities**, e.g. American Depository Receipts.

■ **Units in Collective Investment Schemes** including shares in, or securities of, an Open-Ended Investment Company (OEIC). A collective investment scheme is a specified investment whatever underlying property the scheme invests in.

■ **Rights over a stakeholder pension.**

■ **Options** to acquire or dispose of any specified investment or currencies, gold, silver, platinum or palladium.

■ **Futures** on anything for investment purposes. This differs from the treatment of options as it will cover all futures regardless of the underlying investment, provided it is for investment purposes.

The definition of 'investment purposes' is complex. In general terms, any futures contract traded either on an exchange, or in an over-the-counter market or form similar to that traded on an exchange, will constitute an investment. The type of future, in effect, excluded by this definition would be a short-term contract between a producer and a consumer of a good to purchase that good in the future, e.g. a wheat buyer buying from a farmer. This can sometimes be referred to as a 'commercial purpose future'.

Exam tip

As a rule of thumb, unless the examiner indicates otherwise, you should assume that a future *is* for investment purposes.

■ **Contracts for differences (CFDs).** A contract for a difference is a contract whose price tracks the price of an underlying asset, while the CFD holder does not take ownership of the asset. The underlying asset might be a company's shares, a bond, a currency, a commodity or an index. Investors can use CFDs to take a short position – and thus gain from price declines, but lose if the price rises.

■ **Lloyd's syndicate capacity and membership.** Lloyd's is an insurance institution specialising in risks such as aviation and marine insurance. Insurance is provided by members and syndicates.

■ **Funeral plan contracts.** These are contracts whereby someone pays for their funeral before their death.

- **Regulated mortgages.** Note that not all mortgages are covered, only regulated mortgages. In a regulated mortgage the loan is secured by a first legal mortgage or property located in the UK, which will be occupied (at least 40% of the time) by the borrower or their family.

- **Rights to or interests in specified investments.** 'Repos' (sale and repurchase agreements) in relation to specified investments (e.g. a government bond) are specified investments.

- **Personal pensions.** This is a pension plan which is not a stakeholder scheme and is not an employment-based (occupational) scheme.

- **Home finance.** This covers types of personal mortgage finance.

Spot currency ('forex') trades, general loans (e.g. car loans), property deals and National Savings & Investments products are *not* specified investments.

When applying for authorisation to carry out a regulated activity regarding a specified investment, the firm will specify on the application form which regulated activities relating to which specified investments it wishes to conduct.

4.5 Authorisation routes

Learning objective | **Know** the authorisation procedure for firms: the need for authorisation; the threshold conditions for authorisation

FSMA 2000 has created a single authorisation regime for the regulated activities within its scope. This contrasts with the previous financial services regulation arrangements, which contained a variety of separate regulatory regimes.

A firm may be authorised by one of two main routes:

- Authorisation by the FSA
- Passporting

The concept of a '**passport**' enables a firm to conduct business throughout the EEA. Passporting is discussed in more detail in Chapter 4 of this Study Book.

4.6 Authorisation by the FSA

By far the most common route to authorisation is to obtain permission from the FSA to carry out one or more regulated activities.

The permission that a firm receives will play a crucial role in defining the firm's business scope. This permission is sometimes referred to as **Part IV permission** as it is set out in Part IV of FSMA 2000.

Where a firm obtains permission to do one or more regulated activities, it is then authorised to do those activities. In the application, the applicant must set out which regulated activities and specified investments it requires permission for. The permission will set out what activities and investments are covered and any limitations and requirements that the FSA wishes to impose.

It is not a criminal offence for a firm to go beyond its permission but doing so may give rise to claims from consumers. Furthermore, the FSA will be able to use the full range of disciplinary sanctions, such as cancelling or varying permission.

4.7 Threshold conditions

Before it grants permission, the FSA must be satisfied that the firm is **fit and proper**. In accordance with FSMA 2000, the firm must meet and continue to satisfy the **'threshold conditions'** for the activity concerned in order to be deemed fit and proper. These link closely with the statutory objective of protecting consumers in that they all go towards ensuring that the business will be operated effectively and supervised by the FSA.

There are five threshold conditions (set out in the **COND** part of the FSA Handbook) as follows.

- **Condition 1** sets out the **legal status** that the applicant must have to carry on certain regulated activities, i.e. the legal structure of the business.

- **Condition 2** relates to the **location of the offices** of the applicant. If the applicant is a UK company, its head and registered offices must be located in the UK. For an applicant that is not a company, if it has its head office in the UK, then it must carry on business in the UK.

- **Condition 3** relates to the effect of **close links** of the applicant with other entities, e.g. other members of the same group.

- **Condition 4** requires that the applicant for authorisation must have **adequate resources** for the activities they seek to undertake. Such resources would not only include capital, but also non-financial resources such as personnel.

- **Condition 5.** The final condition relates to the **suitability** of the applicant. The firm must be considered to be 'fit and proper', i.e. it must have integrity, be competent and have appropriate procedures in place to comply with regulations. The management and staff of the firm must also be **competent**.

Exam tip

Use the word **CALLS** to help you to learn the five threshold conditions.

Close links
Adequate resources
Legal status
Location of offices
Suitability

The FSA provides guidance on the threshold conditions in the FSA Handbook. The guidance is unsurprisingly very general, as satisfaction of the threshold conditions is considered on a case-by-case basis in relation to each regulated activity that the firm wishes to carry on.

Note that suitability to carry on **one** regulated activity does not mean that the applicant is suitable to carry on **all** regulated activities.

In determining whether the applicant satisfies and will continue to satisfy the threshold conditions under FSMA 2000, the FSA will consider whether the applicant can demonstrate that the firm is ready, willing and organised to comply with the regulatory obligations that will apply if it is given permission to conduct those regulated activities.

Linking closely to Condition 4 is the requirement that the firm demonstrates that it has adequate **financial resources** to meet the financial resources requirement for its type of firm.

Application procedure

... if a firm wishes to undertake a regulated activity by way of business in the UK, it ... Earlier, we considered the scope of the exemptions (e.g. appointed

...on (**Part IV permission**) from the FSA to do a regulated activity will be ...ng detailed information from the firm and the payment of a fee. The ...on that the applicant will have to submit will be related to the risks posed to ... four regulatory objectives.

... application in accordance with the regulatory objectives and must be proportional in ...requires, having regard to the nature of the applicant's business. Therefore, although ...ts will have to complete all sections of the pack, other sections are specific to certain types ...s. The FSA has **six months** to determine an authorisation from the date of receipt.

...e **information** an applicant must provide includes the following.

- A UK address for the service of documents
- General information about the applicant, intended activities, proposed/current unregulated activities
- How the firm will comply with the regulatory requirements
- Business plan
- Financial budget and projections
- Details of systems to be used including compliance systems
- Details of individuals managing the business, including details of any outsourcing of functions
- For insurance activities, details of the risks being underwritten

The FSA staff will determine whether the threshold conditions have been met including whether the applicant is ready, willing and organised to comply with the regulatory obligations that will apply if it is given permission to conduct those regulated activities. The FSA may, in addition to the information provided, carry out any further enquiries about the applicant, including requiring the applicant to attend meetings to give further information, requiring information supplied to be verified (e.g. by an auditor or accountant) and visiting the applicant's premises. In addition, the FSA may have regard to any person who is connected to the applicant.

Connected persons would include:

- Someone who **controls** the applicant (i.e. owns 20% or more of the shares or who is able to exercise a significant influence over the firm's management). The FSA will determine whether that person is fit and proper to exert influence over the applicant.

- The **directors and partners** of the applicant. Where they are to be approved persons, this would include whether they are fit and proper to be approved for the controlled functions they will be exercising.

- Any **company** in the same group as the applicant.

- Any person with whom the applicant will enter into a material **outsourcing** agreement.

- Any person who may **exert influence** on the applicant, which might pose a risk to the applicant satisfying the threshold conditions.

If the application is successful, permission is granted and the direct consequence is that the applicant is authorised to do those activities. The firm will receive a written notice of the decision and the FSA's register of authorised persons is updated.

The FSA may however, consider that the permissions applied for need to be modified based on the FSA's review of the applicant. They will recommend the application be granted subject to limitations or requirements or to a narrower scope of activities than the applicant originally requested. If the applicant does not accept these limitations or if the FSA simply decide to refuse the application in its entirety then the case is passed to the **Regulatory Decisions Committee (RDC)** for review. The process may result in a final reference to the Financial Services and Markets Tribunal if the RDC's decision is not agreed by the applicant.

4.9 Supervision

Know the supervisory process: purpose of FSA's supervision arrangements; focus on a firm's senior management; FSA's risk-based approach to regulation – ARROW II; FSA's supervisory tools

The FSA's approach to supervision is designed to reflect a number of important concepts.

- The FSA's four **regulatory objectives**.

- The responsibility of **senior management** to ensure that it takes reasonable care to organise and control the affairs of the firm effectively and develops and maintains adequate risk management systems. It is the responsibility of the management to ensure the firm complies with its regulatory requirements.

- The principle that the burden or restriction on firms should be **proportionate** to the benefits to be provided.

The FSA's policy on supervision is grouped under the following **four** headings.

- Diagnostic
- Monitoring
- Preventative
- Remedial

The FSA's overall approach is one of risk-based supervision. The Authority has developed a system known as the **A**djusted **R**isk **R**eturn **O**perating Framework ('**ARROW**'), which involves the FSA looking at particular risks posed by individual firms and also risks to consumers and to the industry as a whole.

ARROW II is a revised model introduced in 2006 and designed to allow FSA supervisors more accurately to reflect their assessment of risk in individual firms or through cross-firm 'thematic' work.

The aim is to focus the FSA's resources in the most efficient and economic way. The FSA will therefore undertake an **impact and probability** assessment on each firm to determine the risks that the firm poses to the four regulatory objectives. In terms of impact, this looks primarily at the impact on the four regulatory objectives. In terms of probability, this is assessed in terms of **risk groups** arising from the firm's strategy, business risks, financial soundness, type of customers, systems and controls and organisation of the firm. The FSA will place firms into risk categories and communicate with them the outcome of the assessment.

The general procedure for this categorisation is as follows.

1. **Preliminary assessment** of the firm's impact on the regulatory objectives
2. **Probability assessment** – the detail will depend on the impact rating and complexity of the firm
3. A sample of various firm's categorisations are then reviewed by a **validation panel**
4. A **letter** is sent to the firm outlining category
5. The FSA ensures **ongoing review** of risk assessment

Certain **individuals** within an authorised firm will require **approval** from the FSA because they carry out **controlled functions**. We explain what the controlled functions are below.

It is important to appreciate that the process of an **individual** obtaining **approved person** status is different from the process of a **firm** obtaining **authorisation**.

To obtain approval, a person must satisfy the FSA that they are **fit and proper** to carry out the controlled function. The suitability of a member of staff who performs a controlled function is covered in the **Fit and Proper Test for Approved Persons** (part of the High Level Standards section of the FSA Handbook).

The most important considerations are as follows.

- **Honesty, integrity and reputation.** The FSA will examine whether the person's reputation might have an adverse impact on the firm they are doing a controlled function for. This will include looking at a number of factors including whether they have had any criminal convictions, civil claims, previous disciplinary proceedings, censure or investigations by any regulator, exchange, governing body or court; any other previous contraventions of regulations; any complaints which have been upheld; any connection with any body which has previously been refused a registration, authorisation or licence or had such registrations, authorisations or licences revoked or been expelled by a regulatory or governmental body; whether they have had any management role within any entities which have gone into liquidation; whether they have been dismissed or asked to resign from a similar position or position of trust; any disqualifications as a director, and finally whether they have been candid and truthful in their dealings with all regulatory bodies and demonstrated a willingness to comply with the regulatory and legal standards applicable to them. When looking at previous convictions, even old (i.e. spent) convictions, as defined in the Rehabilitation of Offenders Act 1974, can be taken into account.

- **Competence and capability.** The FSA will examine whether the Training and Competence requirements in the FSA Handbook have been complied with and whether they have demonstrated by training and experience that they are able to perform the controlled function. If a person has been convicted of, or dismissed or suspended from employment due to drug or alcohol abuse this will be considered in relation only to their continuing ability to perform that function. In addition, S61 FSMA 2000 emphasises that the fit and proper test for approved persons includes assessing qualifications, training and competence. It is not a requirement that a person has experience in order to be approved.

- **Financial soundness.** The FSA will look at whether the applicant has any outstanding judgement debts, has filed for bankruptcy or been involved in any similar proceedings. The fact that a person is of limited financial resources will not in itself affect their suitability to perform a controlled function.

These criteria must be met on a continuing basis. Individuals performing a controlled function must obtain approval **before** they take up the role. Approved persons must adhere to the seven **Statements of Principle**, which are discussed later.

47

To apply for approval the firm must complete **Form A**. It is the responsibility of the firm and not the individual candidate to submit the application. Where a firm outsources a controlled function it must take reasonable care to ensure that no person performs a controlled function regarding the firm's regulated activities without FSA approval. FSMA 2000 allows the FSA **three months** from the time it receives a properly completed application form to come to a decision.

A firm must take reasonable care to ensure that a member of staff does not perform a controlled function unless he has prior approval from the FSA. The firm has a duty to send a notice to withdraw approval on **Form C** within **seven** business days to the FSA if an approved person ceases to perform a controlled function. If the individual is determined to be fit and proper, the FSA will grant the application for approval and provide written notification of this to the firm and will update its register of approved persons. Where the FSA staff decide to refuse a person approved person status, the matter is passed on to the RDC who will deal with the decision. If the applicant is not satisfied by the RDC's decision they can refer the matter to the Financial Services and Markets Tribunal.

4.11 Controlled functions

Learning objective	**Understand** the FSA's controlled functions: the five functional areas, the main roles within each, the four areas of significant influence functions, the requirement for FSA approval prior to appointment

Section 59 FSMA 2000 and the **Supervision Manual (SUP)** states that a person cannot carry out a controlled function in a firm unless that individual has been **approved** by the FSA.

Note that we are now referring to the individual members of staff of an authorised firm. As stated earlier in this chapter, when a person is performing a controlled function and is not approved, there is a breach of statutory duty and a private person has the right to sue their firm for damages if they have suffered loss, using **S71** FSMA 2000.

The FSA may specify a function as a **controlled function** if the individual performing it is:

- Exerting a significant influence on the conduct of the firm's affairs
- Dealing directly with customers
- Dealing with the property of customers

The FSA Handbook (specifically, the **Supervision Manual**) has identified specific controlled functions which are split into the following groups. (The numbering is discontinuous because of re-categorisation of functions.)

Group	Function
	11. Money Laundering Reporting Officer function
	12. Actuarial function
	12A. With-profits actuary function
	12B. Lloyd's actuary function
Systems and controls function	28. Systems and controls function
Significant management function	29. Significant management function
Customer functions	30. Customer function

Individuals who fall within all of the above categories **except** customer functions would be considered to be exerting a **significant influence** on the conduct of the firm's affairs.

4.12 Training and Competence regime

Know the Training and Competence regime: the application of the systems and control responsibilities in relation to the competence of employees; the requirements for Approved Persons; the requirements for staff dealing with retail clients

Principle 3 of the **Principles for Businesses** requires firms to take reasonable care to organise and control its affairs responsibly and effectively, with adequate risk management systems. This implies having appropriate systems of control, including ensuring employees maintain and enhance competence.

SYSC states that a firm's systems and controls should enable it to satisfy itself of the suitability of anyone who acts for it. A requirement under **MiFID** is that firms must employ personnel with the skills, knowledge and expertise necessary for the discharge of the responsibilities allocated to them.

Requirements relating to Training and Competence (TC) for employees are set out in the FSA Handbook, as summarised below.

A contravention of the TC rules does not give rise to a right of action by a private person under section 150 of FSMA 2000.

4.13 The competent employees rule

Competence means having the skills, knowledge and expertise needed to discharge the responsibilities of an employee's role. This includes achieving a good standard of **ethical behaviour**.

- The **competent employees rule** is now the main Handbook requirement relating to the competence of employees. The purpose of the TC sourcebook is to support the FSA's supervisory function by supplementing the competent employees rule for **retail activities**.

- The **competent employees rule** is that firms must employ personnel with the skills, knowledge and expertise necessary for the discharge of the responsibilities allocated to them. This rule applies to non-MiFID firms as well as **MiFID** firms.

4.14 Assessment of competence and supervision

Appropriate examination requirements apply to **designated investment business** carried on for a **retail client**, except that they do not apply to providing basic advice on non-deposit-based stakeholder products. There are also appropriate examination requirements for **regulated mortgage activity**, and home reversion schemes, carried on for customers.

Employees must not carry out these activities without first passing the relevant **regulatory module** of an appropriate examination.

Firms may choose to impose time limits on the time by which examinations must be passed, or on the number of times examinations can be attempted.

In respect of these activities, firms must not allow employees to carry them on without **appropriate supervision**.

The **level and intensity** of supervision should be significantly greater in the period before the firm has assessed the employee as competent, than after. A firm should, therefore, have clear criteria and procedures relating to the **specific point** at which the employee is **assessed as competent** in order to be able to demonstrate when and why a reduced level of supervision may be considered appropriate. At all stages, firms should consider the **level of relevant experience** of an employee when determining the level of supervision required.

Those providing the supervision should have the necessary **coaching and assessment skills**, as well as **technical knowledge**. Firms should consider whether supervisors should themselves pass **appropriate examinations**.

Employees' **training needs** should be assessed at the outset and at regular intervals, including when their role changes. Firms must review employees' competence on a regular and frequent basis, and should take action to ensure that they **remain competent** in their role, taking into account:

- Technical knowledge and its application
- Skills and expertise
- Changes in markets, products, legislation and regulation

4.15 Appropriate examinations

The FSA maintains a list of **appropriate examinations**, for the activities for which they are required, from which firms may choose. Although a firm may set its own examinations, choosing examinations from the FSA list may be relied on as 'tending to establish compliance' with the TC rules.

An employee with three years of 'up-to-date' **relevant experience outside the UK** may be exempted from modules of an appropriate examination, but the regulatory module must still be taken. However, this type of exemption will not apply to those advising retail clients on packaged products, broker fund advising, advising on syndicate participation at Lloyd's or acting as a pension transfer specialist.

4.16 T&C record-keeping

A firm must make appropriate records to demonstrate compliance with the rules in TC and keep them for the following periods after an employee stops carrying on the activity:

- At least five years for MiFID business
- Three years for non-MiFID business, and
- Indefinitely for a pension transfer specialist

> BPP Learning Media cannot provide advice on Appropriate Examination exemptions. This should be discussed with your Compliance Officer, whose responsibility it is to decide which Appropriate Examinations you must take.

4.17 Whistleblowing

- Encourage firms to adopt and communicate procedures for employees to raise concerns about the risk management arrangements of the firm

Whistleblowing is the process whereby a worker seeks to make a **protected disclosure** to a regulator or law enforcement agency outside the firm, in good faith, of information which tends to show that one or more of the following activities is, or is likely, to be committed or is being deliberately concealed by their employer.

- A criminal offence
- A failure to comply with a legal obligation
- A miscarriage of justice
- A breach of health and safety rules
- Damage to the environment

A firm cannot include a clause in the employee's contract preventing the employee from making such a disclosure, i.e. from 'blowing the whistle' on their employer's practices. The rules apply even if the activity listed above occurs outside the UK.

In addition, if the firm or member of staff of an authorised firm were to discriminate against an employee who made a disclosure in any way, the FSA would regard this as a serious matter. In particular the FSA would question the firm's **'suitability'** under **Threshold Condition 5** and the individual's **fitness and propriety**. In serious cases, the FSA could withdraw the firm's authorisation and an individual's approval.

5   MISCELLANEOUS OFFENCES UNDER FSMA 2000

Know the purpose, provisions, offences and defences of S397 FSMA 2000 – Misleading Statements and Practices

Under S397 FSMA 2000 'Misleading Statements and Practices', each of the following is an offence.

- Mislead the market either through a **statement, promise or forecast**. Misleading statements that are intended to make individuals or the market move in a particular direction will constitute an offence if they are made recklessly or with dishonest intent. It is a defence if the statement was made in accordance with the price stabilisation rules.

- Engage in a **course of conduct** which creates a false or misleading impression as to the market, price or value of investments and that is intended to make individuals or the market move in a particular direction. It is a defence if the statement was made in accordance with the price stabilisation rules or the offender reasonably believed a false or misleading impression would not be created by their conduct.

- Dishonestly **conceal** material facts, which may make individuals or the market move in a particular direction.

This is a matter of criminal law which applies to all persons and can be brought to justice either through a Magistrate's Court or through a Crown Court.

Exam tip	You are not required to know the maximum penalty for the exam.

CHAPTER ROUNDUP

- No-one may carry on a regulated activity, unless either authorised, or exempt from authorisation. Some activities (e.g. media coverage, but not tipsheets) are excluded from the authorisation requirement.

- Disciplinary measures include public censure, unlimited fines, restitution orders and cancellation of authorisation or approval. Various Statutory Notices may be issued in cases involving the FSA's Regulatory Decisions Committee.

- The Financial Services and Markets Tribunal can re-hear FSA enforcement and authorisation cases.

- An individual can claim damages for breaches of rules by an authorised firm.

- The FSA has wide powers to visit firms' premises without notice and to require documents to be produced.

- The Regulated Activities Order specifies the list of regulated activities, and the specified investments covered by FSMA 2000.

- A firm may be authorised through obtaining 'Part IV permission' or, for EEA firms, through passporting. Five threshold conditions must be met for authorisation, which is specific to the types of activities the firm carries out.

- The FSA's approach to supervision is 'risk-based', so that supervisory effort is directed at higher risk areas.

- Those carrying out a controlled function need to meet a 'fit and proper' test to be approved persons. This test covers honesty, integrity and reputation; competence and capability; and financial soundness.

- Controlled functions include exerting significant influence on the firm, and dealing with customers or their property.

- A firm is responsible for ensuring that there is appropriate training for employees and that employees remain competent.

- A 'whistleblowing' employee can make a protected disclosure to a regulator or law enforcement agency of wrongdoing.

- It is an offence to mislead the market through a statement, promise or forecast, to create a false market, or to dishonestly conceal material facts which may influence individuals or move the market.

TEST YOUR KNOWLEDGE

2.	What are the penalties for breaching the general prohibition?	
3.	Can you name three types of exempt persons?	▪ ▪ ▪
4.	What is the RDC and what is its role?	
5.	Can you name three excluded activities?	▪ ▪ ▪
6.	Can you name three threshold conditions?	
7.	What is 'ARROW II'?	
8.	What is the difference between authorisation and approval?	
9.	What legislation covers 'whistleblowing'?	
10.	What does S397 FSMA 2000 cover?	

TEST YOUR KNOWLEDGE: ANSWERS

1. Section 19 FSMA 2000 is called the 'general prohibition'. It requires a company to be authorised by the FSA if it is carrying out regulated activities by way of business in the UK (unless it is exempt or excluded).

   (See Section 1.1)

2. Penalties for breach of S19 FSMA 2000 include criminal and civil sanctions. The maximum criminal penalty is two years in prison and/or an unlimited fine (in the Crown Court). Civil penalties include contracts being unenforceable, compensation, injunctions and restitution orders.

   (See Section 1.2)

3. You could have mentioned any three of the following (mnemonic: **April**): **A**ppointed Representatives, **P**rofessional people, **R**IEs, **R**OIEs, **R**CHs, **I**nstitutions, e.g. the Bank of England and **L**loyd's members.

   (See Section 1.7)

4. The RDC is the Regulatory Decisions Committee. The RDC is outside the FSA's management structure and is used to decide on action in disciplinary cases and also withdrawing, varying or refusing authorisation or approval.

   (See Section 2.1)

5. Recall the word **Demote**: **D**ealing as principal where the person is not holding themselves out to the market as willing to deal, **E**mployee share schemes, **M**edia, **O**verseas persons, **T**rustees, nomin**E**es and personal representatives. You could have mentioned any three.

   (See Section 4.3)

6. You could have mentioned any three of: legal status, location of offices, close links, adequate resources and suitability.

   (See Section 4.7)

7. ARROW is the risk-based supervision model which involves the FSA looking at particular risks posed by individual firms and also at risks to consumers and to the industry as a whole. ARROW II is a revised model which is designed to allow FSA supervisors more accurately to reflect their assessment of risk in individual firms or through cross-firm 'thematic' work.

   (See Section 4.9)

8. A firm needs to be authorised under S19 FSMA 2000 if it is carrying out regulated activities by way of business in the UK. An individual requires approval under S59 FSMA 2000 if he/she is undertaking one of the FSA's controlled functions e.g. as director, or compliance oversight.

   (See Sections 1.6, 4.10 and 4.11)

9. The Public Interest Disclosure Act 1998 (PIDA).

   (See Section 4.17)

10. Section 397 FSMA 2000 relates to Misleading Statements and Practices. It covers dishonestly or recklessly making false or misleading statements, dishonestly concealing material facts and engaging in a course of conduct which gives a false or misleading impression.

    (See Section 5)

INTRODUCTION

There are various measures designed to deal with crimes relating to the financial services sector as well as to financial transactions generally. Crimes could be committed by persons within the industry or outside it. In the case of the laundering of proceeds of crime, a criminal may make use of accounts and transactions in ways that financial services employees become aware of.

Measures against financial crime have been stepped up in recent years. It is important to know the law so that one does not inadvertently breach it, as ignorance of the law is not a defence. It is also important to know how legislation and regulations require those working in the financial sector to contribute to the detection and investigation of crime.

We also review in this chapter the provisions relating to data protection.

CHAPTER CONTENTS

LEARNING OBJECTIVES

Insider dealing

- **Understand** the meaning of 'inside information' and 'insider'

- **Understand** the offences described in the legislation and the instruments covered by the Criminal Justice Act 1993

- **Know** the general defences available with regard to insider dealing

- **Know** the special defences: market makers acting in good faith, market information and price stabilisation

- **Know** the FSA's powers to prosecute under insider dealing

Market abuse

- **Understand** the statutory offence of market abuse

- **Know** the status of FSA's Code of Market Conduct; the territorial scope of the legislation and regulation

- **Know** the offences outlined in the Code of Market Conduct

- **Know** the concept of effect rather than intention; the concept of a reasonable regular user

- **Understand** the enforcement regime for market abuse

- **Know** the statutory exceptions (safe harbours) to market abuse

- **Understand** the distinction between offences under market abuse, insider dealing and under S397 Financial Services and Markets Act 2000

- **Understand** the duty of firms to report suspicious transactions

Money laundering

- **Understand** the terms 'money laundering', 'criminal conduct' and 'criminal property' and the application of money laundering to all crimes and the power of the Secretary of State to determine what is 'relevant criminal conduct'

- **Understand** that the UK legislation on money laundering is found in the Proceeds of Crime Act 2002 (POCA 2002) as amended by the Serious Organised Crime and Police Act 2005 (SOCPA 2005), the Money Laundering Regulations 2003, the FSA Senior Management Arrangements, Systems and Controls Sourcebook (SYSC) and that guidance to these provisions is found in the Joint Money Laundering Steering Group Guidance, and **understand** the interaction between them

- **Understand** the main offence set out in the Money Laundering Regulations (internal controls), which includes obligations on firms for adequate training of individuals on money laundering

- **Understand** the three stages of money laundering

- **Understand** the main offences of assistance, i.e. concealing, arrangements, acquisition, use and possession; failure to report; tipping off; and the implications of Part 7 POCA 2002 regarding the objective test in relation to reporting suspicious transactions; that appropriate disclosure (internal for staff and to SOCA) for the firm is a defence

- **Understand** the new principles-based approach adopted by the FSA in August 2006 as covered by the Senior Management Arrangements, Systems and Controls Sourcebook (SYSC)

    - Need for risk assessment
    - Need for high level policy statement
    - Detailed procedures implementing the firm's risk based approach

- **Understand** the Money Laundering aspects of know your customer (Joint Money Laundering Steering Groups' Guidance for the Financial Sector)

- **Understand** the importance of being able to recognise a suspicious transaction and the requirement for staff to report to the MLRO and for the firm to report to the Serious Organised Crime Agency (SOCA)

- **Know** what activities are regarded as 'terrorism' in the UK (Terrorism Act 2000 Part 1)

- **Understand** the importance of preventative measures in respect of terrorist financing and the essential differences between laundering the proceeds of crime and the financing of terrorist acts

- **Know** the obligations laid on regulated firms under S18 and S19 (1)(2)(3)(4)(7) Terrorism Act 2000: money laundering of terrorist funds and duty to report; and the Anti-Terrorism, Crime and Security Act 2001, Schedule 2, Part 3 (disclosure of information) and where to find the sanction list for terrorist activities

- **Understand** the interaction between the rules of FSA, the above legislation and the JMLSG Guidance regarding terrorism

Model Code for Directors

- **Know** the main purpose and provisions of the FSA's Model Code in relation to Director's dealings, including closed periods, Chairman's approval, no short-term dealing

Data Protection Act 1998

- **Know** the eight Data Protection principles, the need for notification of data controllers with the Information Commissioner; the record-keeping requirements of FSA regulated firms

1 INSIDER DEALING

Learning objective | **Understand** the offences described in the legislation and the instruments covered by the Criminal Justice Act 1993

1.1 Introduction

Insider dealing is the offence of acting with information that is not freely and openly available to all other participants in the market place. This became an offence in 1980 but the current legislation making it a criminal offence is found in **Part V** of the **Criminal Justice Act 1993**.

The Act makes it a **criminal offence** for connected persons who receive inside information to act on that information.

The legislation (Schedule 2) covers the following instruments.

- Shares
- Debt securities issued by the private or public sector
- Warrants
- Depository receipts
- Options, futures or contracts for a difference on any of the above

1.2 Insider

Learning objective | **Understand** the meaning of 'inside information' and 'insider'

An insider is defined under CJA 1993 as an individual who has **information** in his possession that he **knows** is **inside information** and **knows** is from an **inside source**.

Inside information in this context refers to **unpublished price-sensitive information** that is **specific or precise** and **relates to a security or its issuer**.

What is **published** information? The following information is deemed to be 'published'.

- Information published via a regulated market, e.g. an RIE
- Information contained in public records
- Information which can otherwise be readily acquired by market users, e.g. in the financial press
- Information derived from public information
- Information which can only be acquired by expertise or by payment of a fee
- Information which is published only to a section of the public, rather than the public in general, or published outside the UK
- Information which can be acquired by observation, e.g. a factory burning down

An inside source is **an individual** and would include a **director, employee** or **shareholder** of an issuer of securities or a person having access to the information by virtue of their employment, office or profession.

A person will also be an inside source if he receives the information directly or indirectly from one of the above and satisfies the general definition above.

1.3 Offences

1.4 General defences

1.4 General defences

| earning objective | **Know** the general defences available with regard to insider dealing |

An individual is not guilty of insider **dealing** if he can show that:

- He did not, at the time, expect the dealing to result in a profit attributable to the fact that the information was price sensitive

- At the time, he believed on reasonable grounds that the information had been disclosed widely enough to ensure that none of those taking part in the dealing would be prejudiced by not having the information

- He would have done what he did even if he had not had the information

A similar series of defences are available to the charge of **encouraging** another to deal in price-affected securities.

An individual is not guilty of insider dealing by virtue of a **disclosure** of information if he shows that:

- He did not, at the time, expect any person, because of the disclosure, to deal in securities either through a regulated market or via a professional intermediary

- Although he had such an expectation at the time, he did not expect the dealing to result in a profit attributable to the fact that the information was price sensitive in relation to the securities

1.5 Special defences

| earning objective | **Know** the special defences: market makers acting in good faith, market information and price stabilisation |

1.5.1 Market makers

A market maker is a person who holds himself out at all normal times in compliance with the rules of a RIE as willing to acquire or dispose of securities and is required to do so under those rules. An individual is not guilty of insider dealing by virtue of dealing in securities or encouraging another to deal if he can show that he acted in **good faith** in the course of market making.

1.5.2 Market information

An individual is not guilty of an offence under the Act if he can show that the information which he had as an insider was **market information** (information concerning transactions in securities that either have been or are about to be undertaken) and that it was reasonable for an individual in his position to have acted in that manner when in possession of inside information. Consideration will be taken as to the content of the information, the circumstances of receiving the information and the capacity in which the recipient acts, to determine whether it is reasonable.

This defence will also cover the **facilitation of takeover bids**.

1.5.3 Price stabilisation

An individual is not guilty of an offence under the Act by virtue of dealing in securities or encouraging another person to deal if he can show that he acted in conformity with the **price stabilisation rules**.

1.6 Prosecution by the FSA

Know the FSA's powers to prosecute under insider dealing

The FSA has powers under S401 and S402 FSMA 2000 to prosecute a range of criminal offences, including **insider dealing**, in England, Wales and Northern Ireland.

While the Department of Business, Enterprise and Regulatory Reform (formerly the Department of Trade and Industry) retain their powers to prosecute, since 2001 the **FSA** will now normally prosecute insider dealing. Accordingly, the London Stock Exchange (as the person who often initiates an investigation) will pass information directly to the FSA.

2 MARKET ABUSE

Know the status of the FSA's Code of Conduct; the territorial scope of the legislation and regulation

Know the offences outlines in the Code of Market Conduct

Know the concept of effect rather than intention; the concept of a reasonable regular user

2.1 Introduction

Market abuse is a **civil offence** under **S118 FSMA 2000,** which provides an alternative civil regime for enforcing the criminal prohibitions on insider dealing and misleading statements/practices.

The UK market abuse rules conform with the **EU Market Abuse Directive**.

The **territorial scope** of market abuse is very wide. It covers everyone, not just authorised firms and approved persons. Firms or persons outside the UK are also covered by the offence.

As market abuse is a **civil offence**, the FSA must prove, on the balance of probabilities, that a person:

- Engaged in market abuse, or
- By taking or refraining from action, required or encouraged another person to engage in market abuse

As shown in the diagram opposite, there are seven types of behaviour that can amount to market abuse.

Behaviour

Which falls into one or more of the types of behaviour

- Insider Dealing
- Improper Disclosure
- Misuse of Information
- Manipulating Transactions
- Manipulating Devices
- Dissemination
- Misleading Behaviour and Distortion

2.2 Requiring and encouraging

Section 123(1)(b) FSMA 2000 allows the FSA to impose penalties on a person who, by taking or refraining from taking any action, has required or encouraged another person or persons to engage in behaviour, which if engaged in by A, would amount to market abuse.

The following are **examples** of behaviour that might fall within the scope of section 123(1)(b).

- A director of a company, while in possession of inside information, instructs an employee of that company to deal in qualifying investments or related investments in respect of which the information is inside information. (This could amount to **requiring**.)

- A person recommends or advises a friend to engage in behaviour which, if he himself engaged in it, would amount to market abuse. (This could be **encouraging** market abuse.)

2.3 The regular market user test

A regular user is a **hypothetical reasonable person** who regularly deals on that market in investments of the kind in question. The **regular market user test** then determines in light of the circumstances whether an offence has been committed.

Since the implementation of the Market Abuse Directive, the regular market user is only used to determine whether market abuse has occurred in relation to the behaviours 'Misuse of Information', 'Misleading Behaviour' and 'Distortion'.

Therefore, the regular market user decides:

■   Whether information that is not generally available would be relevant when deciding which transactions in qualifying investments or related investments should be undertaken, and

■   Whether behaviour is below the expected standard, or creates a false or misleading impression or distorts the market

2.4 Qualifying investments and prescribed markets

Behaviour will only constitute market abuse if it occurs **in the UK or in relation to qualifying investments traded on a prescribed market**. The term 'behaviour' is specifically mentioned as the offence of market abuse can cover both action and inaction.

A **prescribed market** means any UK RIE, and any regulated market. **Qualifying investment** thus means any investment traded on a UK RIE or a regulated market. **Regulated markets** comprise the main EEA exchanges.

The definition of prescribed market and qualifying investment are amended slightly with reference to the offences of '**Misuse of Information**', '**Misleading Behaviour**' and '**Distortion**'. Here, a prescribed market means any UK RIE. Qualifying investment thus means any investment traded on a UK RIE. Therefore, these offences are only relevant to the UK markets.

In addition, the rules confirm that a prescribed market accessible electronically in the UK would be treated as operating in the UK.

As behaviour must be **in relation to** qualifying investments, the regime is not limited to on-market dealings. A transaction in an OTC (Over The Counter) derivative contract on a traded security or commodity would be covered by the regime. In addition, abusive trades on foreign exchanges could constitute market abuse if the underlying instrument also trades on a prescribed market. This makes the regime much wider than the criminal law offences.

2.5 The definition of market abuse

Market abuse is behaviour, whether by one person alone or by two or more persons jointly or in concert, which occurs in relation to:

■   Qualifying investments admitted to trading on a prescribed market, or

■   Qualifying investments in respect of which a request for admission to trading on a prescribed market has been made, or

■   Related investments of a qualifying investment (strictly, this is only relevant to the offences of 'Insider Dealing' and 'Improper Disclosure' – see below)

and falls within one or more of the offences below.

2.6 The seven types of market abuse offence

Learning objectives   **Understand** the statutory offence of market abuse

Understand the distinction between offences under market abuse, insider dealing and under the Financial Services and Markets Act 2000, S397

BPP
LEARNING MEDIA

The seven types of behaviour that can constitute market abuse are as follows:

1   **Insider Dealing**. This is where an insider deals, or attempts to deal ...

the terms on which transactions in qualifying investments should be effected, and

–   Likely to be regarded by a regular user of the market as a failure on the part of the person concerned to observe the standard of behaviour reasonably expected of a person in his position.

4   **Manipulating Transactions**. This consists of effecting transactions or orders to trade (otherwise than for legitimate reasons and in conformity with accepted market practices) which

–   Give, or are likely to give a false or misleading impression as to the supply, demand or price of one or more qualifying investments, or

–   Secure the price of one or more such investments at an abnormal or artificial level.

5   **Manipulating Devices**. This consists of effecting transactions or orders to trade which employ fictitious devices or any other form of deception.

6   **Dissemination**. This consists of the dissemination of information by any means which gives, or is likely to give, a false or misleading impression as to a qualifying investment by a person who knew or could reasonably be expected to have known that the information was false or misleading.

7   **Misleading Behaviour** and **Distortion**. This fills any gaps in '4', '5' and '6' above and is where the behaviour

–   Is likely to give a regular user of the market a false or misleading impression as to the supply of, demand for, or price or value of, qualifying investments, or

–   Would be regarded by a regular user of the market as behaviour that would distort the market in such an investment and is likely to be regarded by a regular user of the market as a failure on the part of the person concerned to observe the standard of behaviour reasonably expected of a person in his position.

2.7 Intention

The market abuse regime is **effects based** rather than 'intent based'. Thus, whether the perpetrator intended to abuse the market is largely irrelevant – the key question is whether the action **did** abuse the market.

2.8 Code of Market Conduct

While the law is set out in FSMA, the FSA also has a duty to draft a **Code of Market Conduct**.

The main provisions of the Code of Market Conduct are that it sets out:

■   Descriptions of behaviour that, in the opinion of the FSA, do or do not amount to market abuse. Descriptions of behaviour which do not amount to market abuse are called '**safe harbours**'

■   Descriptions of behaviour that are or are not **accepted market practices** in relation to one or more identified markets

- Factors that, in the opinion of the FSA, are to be taken into account in determining whether or not behaviour amounts to market abuse

The Code does not exhaustively describe all types of behaviour that may or may not amount to market abuse.

2.9 Enforcement and penalties

Learning objective   **Understand** the enforcement regime for market abuse

The FSA may impose one or more of the following **penalties** on those found to have committed market abuse.

- An unlimited **fine**

- Issue a **public statement**

- Apply to the court to seek an **injunction** or **restitution order**

- Where an authorised/approved person is guilty of market abuse, they will also be guilty of a breach of the FSA's Principles and they could, in addition to the above penalties, have disciplinary proceedings brought against them, which may result in withdrawal of authorisation/approval.

The case of Paul Davidson ('The Plumber') has led to change in perceptions about how market abuse may be treated. The current position is that a **civil standard of proof** (on the balance of probabilities) of the appropriate degree can still be used by the FSA in market abuse cases. However, even when the punishment (in accordance with S123 FSMA 2000) is treated as **civil** for domestic law purposes, market abuse is a **criminal** charge (with a standard of proof 'beyond reasonable doubt') for the purposes of the European Convention on Human Rights, and someone committing it is subject to possible criminal prosecution.

In addition to being able to impose penalties for market abuse, the FSA is given criminal prosecution powers to enforce insider dealing and S397. The FSA has indicated that it will not pursue both the civil and criminal regime. In terms of the enforcement process for market abuse, this is the same as FSA's disciplinary process.

2.10 Safe harbours

Learning objective   **Know** the statutory exceptions (safe harbours) to market abuse

If a person is within one of the **safe harbours** set out in the **Code of Market Conduct** they are not committing market abuse. These are indicated by the letter **C** in the Handbook.

Generally, there are no rules in the Takeover Code that permit or require a person to behave in a way which amounts to market abuse.

However, the following rules provide a **safe harbour** meaning that behaviour conforming with that rule does not amount to market abuse.

2.10.1 FSA rules

Behaviour caused by the proper operation of a Chinese wall or behaviour that relates to the timing, dissemination or content to a disclosure under the Listing Rules will not amount to market abuse.

2.10.2 Takeover Code

~~Behaviour conforming with~~

However, buy-back programmes which do not follow the Buy-Back and Stabilisation Regulation are not automatically seen as market abuse, but do not have an automatic safe harbour.

2.11 Due diligence defence

Under Section 123 FSMA 2000, the FSA may not impose a financial penalty in relation to market abuse where it is satisfied that the person believed, on reasonable grounds, that his behaviour did not amount to market abuse or he took all reasonable precautions and exercised all **due diligence** to avoid engaging in market abuse.

2.12 Notification of suspicious transactions by firms

earning objective   **Understand** the duty of firms to report suspicious transactions

The FSA's Supervision manual (**SUP**) stipulates that an authorised **firm** which:

- Arranges or executes a transaction with or for a client in a qualifying investment admitted to trading on a prescribed market, and

- Has reasonable grounds to suspect that the transaction might constitute market abuse

must **notify the FSA** without delay.

3   MONEY LAUNDERING

arning objectives   **Understand** the terms money laundering, criminal conduct and criminal property and the application of money laundering to all crimes and the power of the Secretary of State to determine what is 'relevant criminal conduct'

Understand that the UK legislation on money laundering is found in the Proceeds of Crime Act 2002 (POCA 2002) as amended by the Serious Organised Crime and Police Act 2005 (SOCPA 2005), the Money Laundering Regulations 2003, the FSA Senior Management Arrangements, Systems and Controls Sourcebook (SYSC) and that guidance to these provisions is found in the Joint Money Laundering Steering Group Guidance Notes and understand the interaction between them

3.1 Introduction

Money laundering is the process by which money and other property from criminal conduct is made to appear legally derived. By a variety of methods, the nature, source and ownership of those criminal proceeds are concealed.

Criminal conduct is any crime that constitutes an offence in the UK, or any act abroad that would constitute an offence if it had occurred in the UK.

Property is criminal property if it constitutes a person's benefit from criminal conduct and the alleged offender knows or suspects that it constitutes this benefit.

This means that UK Money Laundering legislation applies to the proceeds of all crimes no matter how small.

Learning objective **Understand** the three stages of money laundering

The three stages of money laundering can be broken down as follows.

- **Placement** – the investment of the proceeds of criminal activity
- **Layering** – the mingling of the money from an illegal source with that from a legitimate source
- **Integration** – the withdrawal and usage of the now undetectable proceeds of criminal activity

The consequence is that the origin of and entitlement to the money are disguised and the money can again be used to benefit the criminal and/or his associates.

In recognition of the scale and impact of money laundering internationally various national governments have in recent years collaborated on an international scale to combat money laundering. Action taken has concentrated not only on the law enforcement process but also on recommendations to banks and financial institutions to put in place practices and procedures which will assist in the detection of money laundering activity.

3.2 Money Laundering Directives

In 1991, the European Union adopted Council Directive 91/308 on prevention of the use of the financial system for the purpose of money laundering. This Directive was implemented by all member states. The **European Union Money Laundering Directive** stipulates that EU member states should ensure that all financial and credit institutions located within the national member states should implement certain **internal procedures** and controls and also ensure that it is a **criminal offence** for individuals to assist money laundering.

In 2001, a **second EU Money Laundering Directive** was adopted to cure some of the deficiencies in the first Directive. A **third EU Money Laundering Directive** is due to be implemented by **15 December 2007**.

In the UK, the internal procedures requirement was implemented by passing the Money Laundering Regulations 1993 (and 2001), which (in line with the second EU Directive) have been replaced by the **Money Laundering Regulations 2003**.

The aims of those internal procedures are threefold.

- **Deterrence** – to prevent credit and financial institutions being used for money laundering purposes

- **Co-operation** – to ensure that there is co-operation between credit and financial institutions and law enforcement agencies

- **Detection** – to establish customer identification and record-keeping procedures within all financial and credit institutions that will assist the law enforcement agencies in detecting, tracing and prosecuting money launderers

The Money Laundering Directive also requires that there be legislation applicable to individuals. The **Proceeds of Crime Act 2002 (POCA)** consolidated and updated the original money laundering requirements which applied to individuals and is now the main legislation covering individual liability.

3.3 The Proceeds of Crime Act 2002: Individual liability

- ~~Assistance~~
- **Failure to report**
- **Tipping off**

3.3.1 Assistance (POCA S327, S328, S329)

The offence

If any person knowingly helps another person to launder the proceeds of criminal conduct, he or she will be committing an offence. This covers obtaining, concealing, disguising, transferring, acquiring, possessing, investing or using the proceeds of crime. The legislation historically covered the laundering of the proceeds of **serious crime**, however as a result of the POCA it now covers the proceeds of **all crimes**, no matter how small. This could include evasion of tax.

The possible defences

- It is a defence to the above offence that a person **disclosed** his knowledge or belief concerning the origins of the property either to the police or to the appropriate officer in his firm.

- Under changes made by the **Serious Organised Crime and Police Act 2005 (SOCPA)**, there may also be a defence if the person knew or believed on reasonable grounds that the relevant criminal conduct occurred outside the UK and the conduct was not at the time unlawful in the overseas jurisdiction.

The penalty

The maximum penalties for any offence of assisting a money launderer are **14 years' imprisonment and/or an unlimited fine**.

3.3.2 Failure to report

The offence

If a person discovers information during the course of his employment that makes him **believe or suspect** money laundering is occurring, he must inform the police or the appropriate officer (usually the Money Laundering Reporting Officer (MLRO)) of the firm as soon as possible. If he fails to make the report as soon as is reasonably practicable, he commits a criminal offence.

For those working in the **regulated sector** (for an authorised firm), this offence covers not only where the person had actual suspicion of laundering (i.e. subjective suspicions) but also where there were **reasonable grounds for being suspicious**. The grounds are when a hypothetical **reasonable person** would in the circumstances have been suspicious (i.e. **objective suspicions**).

The possible defences

The only defences to this charge are if a person charged can prove one of the following.

- He had a **reasonable excuse** for failing to disclose this information. Whether an excuse is reasonable will depend on the circumstances of the case, but it is noteworthy that the person charged has the burden of proving that he had a reasonable excuse for his failure to disclose.

- Where the person had no subjective suspicion but is deemed to have objective suspicions, they had not been provided by their employer with appropriate **training** to recognise and report suspicions.

- Under changes made by the Serious Organised Crime and Police Act 2005 (SOCPA), there may also be a defence if the person knew or believed on reasonable grounds that the relevant criminal conduct occurred outside the UK and the conduct was not at the time unlawful in the overseas jurisdiction.

The relevant legislation specifically provides that any person making a disclosure of this kind will not be in breach of any **duty of confidentiality** owed to a customer.

The penalty

This offence is punishable with a maximum of **five years' imprisonment** and/or an **unlimited fine**.

3.3.3 Tipping off (POCA S333)

The offence

If a person either knows or believes that the police are or will be investigating the laundering of the proceeds of criminal conduct that person **must not disclose to any third party** any information which might prejudice such an investigation. If he does, he will commit the offence of tipping off. This covers the proceeds of **all** crimes no matter how small.

The possible defence

It is a defence to this offence if the person charged can prove that he neither knew nor suspected that the disclosure would prejudice an investigation.

Again, the burden of proving the defence rests upon the person who has been charged with an offence.

The penalty

Tipping off is punishable with a maximum of **five years' imprisonment** and/or an **unlimited fine**.

3.4 Money Laundering Regulations 2003: Institutional liability

Learning objective | **Understand** the main offence set out in the Money Laundering Regulations (internal controls), which includes obligations as firms for adequate training of individuals on money laundering

The Money Laundering Regulations require internal procedures and controls to be implemented to deter criminals from using financial institutions to launder money. This should also enable money laundering to be more easily detected and prosecuted by the law enforcement agencies. The Regulations apply to all firms and individuals authorised to conduct regulated activities under FSMA 2000, as well as to other **relevant businesses**, such as bureaux de change, lawyers, casinos and estate agents.

The following internal systems must be established.

- **Internal reporting procedures** involving the appointment of an officer of the firm to act as Money Laundering Reporting Officer

- **Identification procedures** (unless an exception applies) and **know your customer** requirements

- **Record-keeping procedures** whereby relevant records of transactions must be kept for a minimum of **five years** after the relationship with the customer has ended

- **Adequate training programmes** for all relevant employees

There is a requirement to obtain satisfactory **identification** of all applicants for business as soon as is reasonably practical after initial contact and normally before establishing a business relationship with them.

- Where a customer's identity cannot be verified satisfactorily, the firm must not proceed further with the transaction or the business relationship.

A firm does not need to verify the identity of any of the following.

- A firm carrying out financial services business which is subject to the Money Laundering Regulations, the EU Money Laundering Directive or overseas legislation which contains comparable provisions to those contained in the EU Money Laundering Directive

- One-off or series of linked transactions together less than €15,000

- Individuals taking out certain life insurance contracts without an investment content (general insurance is not exempt)

Note that a firm must verify the identity of a client where it is **suspicious** even if the client technically falls into one of the exceptions listed above.

The following are examples of suspicious activity and are also relevant examples of what is suspicious for the requirement to report suspicions under the individual liability of 'Failure to Report'. (This list is not exhaustive as methods of money laundering evolve through time.)

- No discernible need to use the firm
- Unnecessary use of an intermediary
- Reluctant verification
- Unusual trading patterns
- Introduction from a suspicious jurisdiction
- Non-market price transactions
- Use of bearer securities
- Payments to third parties

In addition to the identification requirements, a firm needs to ensure that it **knows its customer**. This means obtaining an understanding of your client's proposed patterns of trading which will enable the firm to identify any suspicious changes in a client's activities. The types of information a firm may obtain include details regarding the **nature and level of business** to be conducted and the expected **origin of funds** the client is using. What information is required will depend upon the application of commercial judgement by the firm in the circumstances. Any information obtained must be kept up to date by the firm.

Failure to implement these measures is a criminal offence, punishable with a maximum sentence of **two years' imprisonment for any senior officer of the firm and/or an unlimited fine**, irrespective of whether money laundering has taken place.

3.5 Internal reporting procedures

All institutions must appoint an 'appropriate person' within the organisation, generally known as the **Money Laundering Reporting Officer (MLRO)**. The MLRO must then decide whether to report these on to the Serious Organised Crime Agency (SOCA), formerly the National Criminal Intelligence Service (NCIS).

The functions of the MLRO are as follows.

- To receive reports of transactions giving rise to knowledge or suspicion of money laundering activities from employees of the institution

- To determine whether the report of a suspicious transaction from the employee, considered together with all other relevant information, does actually give rise to knowledge or suspicion of money laundering

- If, after consideration, he knows or suspects that money laundering is taking place, to report those suspicions to the appropriate law enforcement agency

For the purpose of each individual employee, making a report made to the MLRO concerning a transaction means that the employee has fulfilled his statutory obligations and will have **no criminal liability** in relation to any money laundering offence in respect of the reported transaction.

3.6 FSA senior management arrangements, systems and controls (SYSC)

Learning objective | **Understand** the new Principles based approach adopted by the FSA in August 2006 as covered by the Senior Management Arrangements, Systems and Controls (SYSC), in particular, the systems and controls that the FSA expects firms to have adopted, the role of the Money Laundering Reporting Officer, Nominated Officer and the compliance function

3.6.1 Systems and controls in relation to compliance, financial crime and money laundering

A firm must take reasonable care to establish and maintain effective systems and controls for compliance with applicable regulations and for countering the risk that the firm might be used to further financial crime. Applicable regulations include the Proceeds of Crime Act 2002, the Money Laundering Regulations 2003 and the Terrorism Act 2000.

The **principles-based approach to regulation**, as we have seen, implies that, instead of formulating very detailed rules, the FSA expects firms to work out for themselves how the Principles for Businesses can be given effect in the firm's business.

The systems and controls laid down should enable the firm to identify, assess, monitor and manage **money laundering risk**, which is, the risk that a firm may be used to further money laundering. In addition, the systems and controls should be **comprehensive** and **proportionate** to the **nature**, **scale** and **complexity** of its activities and be regularly assessed to ensure they remain adequate. Failure by a firm to manage money laundering risk will effectively increase the risk to society of crime and terrorism.

In identifying its **money laundering risk** and in establishing the nature of the systems and controls required, a firm should consider a range of factors, including:

- Its customer, product and activity profiles
- Its distribution channels
- The complexity and volume of its transactions
- Its processes and systems
- Its operating environment

The SYSC rules require firms to ensure that their systems and controls include:

- Allocation to a director or senior manager (who may also be the money laundering reporting officer

- Appropriate **documentation** of its risk management policies and risk profile in relation to money laundering, including documentation of its application of those policies

- Appropriate measures to ensure that **money laundering risk** is taken into account in its day-to-day operation e.g. in the development of new products, the taking on of new customers and changes in its business profile

- Appropriate measures to ensure that **identification procedures** for customers do not unreasonably deny access to its services

3.6.2 The Money Laundering Reporting Officer (MLRO)

The MLRO which each authorised firm must appoint has responsibility for oversight of its compliance with the FSA's SYSC rules on money laundering.

The MLRO:

- Must act as the focal point for all activity within the firm relating to anti-money laundering
- Must have a level of authority and independence within the firm
- Must have access to sufficient resources and information to enable them to carry out that responsibility
- Should be based in the UK

3.6.3 The nominated officer

A **nominated officer** is someone who has been nominated by their employer to receive reports of suspected money laundering. In practice this will be the **Money Laundering Reporting Officer (MLRO)** or **his deputy**.

Employers will have reporting processes in place for staff with suspicions to disclose to the MLRO. The nominated officer will act as a filter for reporting, and is placed under a duty to disclose to the **Serious Organised Crime Agency (SOCA)**, if he knows or suspects, or has reasonable grounds to suspect, that another person is engaged in money laundering.

3.6.4 The compliance function

Depending on the nature, scale and complexity of its business, it may be appropriate for a firm to have a separate **compliance function**. The organisation and responsibilities of the compliance function should be documented.

The compliance function should:

- Be staffed by an appropriate number of competent staff who are sufficiently independent to perform their duties objectively

- Have unrestricted access to the firm's relevant records

- Have ultimate recourse to its governing body

A firm which carries on designated investment business with or for customers must allocate to a director or senior manager the function of having responsibility for oversight of the firm's compliance and reporting to the governing body in respect of that responsibility. This will be the person carrying out the controlled function '**Compliance oversight**' under the FSA's approved persons regime. As a minimum, this individual will have to oversee compliance with COB, CASS and COLL, however, firms are free to give additional responsibilities to this person.

3.7 Joint Money Laundering Steering Group Guidance 2006

Learning objective	**Understand** the standards expected by the 2006 JMLSG Guidance Notes particularly in relation to: risk-based approach; requirements for directors and senior managers to be responsible for money laundering precautions; need for risk assessment; need for high level policy statement; detailed procedures implementing the firm's risk-based approach

3.7.1 Status

The courts must take account of industry guidance, such as the Joint Money Laundering Steering Group (JMLSG) Guidance Notes, which have been approved by a Treasury Minister when deciding whether:

- A person has committed the offence of failing to report money laundering under POCA

- A person has failed to report terrorist financing under the Terrorism Act, or

- A person or institution has failed to comply with any of the requirements of the Money Laundering Regulations 2003

When considering whether to take disciplinary action against an FSA authorised firm for a breach of SYSC, the FSA will have regard to whether a firm has followed relevant provisions in the JMLSG Guidance Notes. The guidance will therefore be significant for individuals or companies subject to regulatory action.

The Guidance Notes provide a sound basis for firms to meet their legislative and regulatory obligations when tailored by firms to their particular business risk profile. Departures from good industry practice, and the rationale for so doing, should be documented and may have to be justified to the FSA.

3.7.2 Directors' and senior managers' responsibility for money laundering precautions

Senior management of FSA authorised firms must provide direction to, and oversight of, the firm's **anti-money laundering (AML)** and **combating the financing of terrorism (CFT)** systems and controls.

Senior management in FSA authorised firms have a responsibility to ensure that the firm's control processes and procedures are appropriately designed, implemented and effectively operated to manage the firm's risks. This includes the risk of the firm being used to further financial crime.

3.7.3 High level policy statement and risk-based approach

The FSA requires authorised firms to produce adequate documentation of its risk management policies and risk profile in relation to money laundering, including documentation of the application of those policies.

A statement of the firm's AML/CFT policy and the procedures to implement it will clarify how the firm's senior management intend to discharge their legal responsibility. This will provide a framework of direction to the firm and its staff, and will identify named individuals and functions responsible for implementing particular aspects of the policy. The policy will also set out how senior management makes its assessment of the money laundering and terrorist financing risks the firm faces, and how these risks are to be managed.

The **policy statement** should be tailored to the circumstances of the firm as the use of a generic document might reflect adversely on the level of consideration given by senior management to the firm's particular risk profile.

The policy statement might include, but is not limited to, the following.

Guiding principles
A statement of the culture and values to be adopted and disseminated throughout the firm towards the prevention of financial crime
A commitment to ensuring that customers' identities will be satisfactorily verified before the firm accepts them
A commitment to the firm 'knowing its customers' appropriately at acceptance and throughout the business relationship
A commitment to ensuring that staff are trained and made aware of the law and their obligations under it
Recognition of the importance of staff promptly reporting their suspicions internally

Risk mitigation approach
A summary of the firm's approach to assessing and managing its money laundering and terrorist financing risk
Allocation of responsibilities to specific persons and functions
A summary of the firm's procedures for carrying out appropriate identification and monitoring checks on the basis of their risk-based approach
A summary of the appropriate monitoring arrangements in place to ensure that the firm's policies and procedures are being carried out

3.7.4 Identifying and assessing the risks faced by the firm

Many customers, by their nature or through what is already known about them by the firm, carry a lower money laundering or terrorist financing risk.

These might include customers:

- Who are employed by, or with a regular source of income from, a known source, e.g. pensioners which supports the activity being undertaken

- With a long-term and active business relationship with the firm

- Represented by those whose appointment is subject to court approval, e.g. executors

Firms should not, however, judge the level of risk solely on the nature of the customer **or** the product **but as a combination of the two**. Firms need to be aware that allowing a higher risk customer to acquire a lower risk product or service on the basis of a verification standard that is appropriate to that lower risk product or service, can lead to a requirement for further verification. This is particularly the case if the customer wishes subsequently to acquire a higher risk product or service.

3.7.5 Money laundering and 'Know Your Customer'

Learning objective

Understand the Money Laundering aspects of know your customer (Joint Money Laundering Steering Groups' Guidance for the Financial Sector)

Firms are expected to 'know their customers'. The **Know Your Customer (KYC)** requirements:

- Help the firm, at the time customer due diligence is carried out, to be reasonably satisfied that customers are who they say they are, to know whether they are acting on behalf of others, whether there are any government sanctions against serving the customer, and

- Assist law enforcement with information on customers or activities under investigation.

The JMLSG Guidance states that, based on an **assessment of the money laundering / terrorist financing risk** that each customer presents, the firm will need to:

- **Verify the customer's identity (ID)** – determining exactly who the customer is

- **Collect additional 'KYC' information**, and keep such information **current and valid** – to understand the customer's circumstances and business, and (where appropriate) the sources of funds or wealth, or the purpose of specific transactions

4 TERRORISM

4.1 Terrorist activities

Learning objectives	**Know** what activities are regarded as 'terrorism' in the UK (Terrorism Act 2000 Part 1)
	Understand the importance of preventative measures in respect of terrorist financing and the essential differences between laundering the proceeds of crime and the financing of terrorist acts

Acts of terrorism committed since 2001 have led to an increase in international efforts to locate and cut off funding for terrorists and their organisations. Terrorists are using increasingly sophisticated methods to transfer funds and often require the services of bankers, accountants and lawyers.

There is a considerable overlap between the movement of terrorist funds and the laundering of criminal assets. Terrorist groups are also known to have well-established links with organised criminal activity. However, there are two major differences between terrorist and criminal funds.

- Often only small amounts are required to commit a terrorist atrocity, therefore increasing the difficulty of tracking the funds.

- Whereas money laundering relates to the proceeds of crime, terrorists can be funded from legitimately obtained income.

The **Terrorism Act 2000** defines **terrorism** in the UK as the use or threat of action wherever it occurs, designed to influence a government or to intimidate the public for the purpose of advancing a political, religious or ideological cause where the action:

- Involves serious violence against a person, or

- Involves serious damage to property, or

- Endangers a person's life, or

- Creates a serious risk to the health or safety of the public, or

- Is designed seriously to interfere with, or seriously to disrupt an electronic system, e.g. a computer virus

4.2 Offences

person of terrorist property by means of concealment, removal from the jurisdiction, transfer to nominees or in any other way

An offence will be committed if the action or possession of terrorist funds occurs in the UK. It will also be an offence if the action or possession occurs outside the UK but would have constituted an offence in the UK if it had occurred here.

4.3 Terrorist property

Terrorist property is defined as money or other property which is likely to be used for the purposes of terrorism, proceeds of the commission of acts of terrorism and proceeds of acts carried out for the purposes of terrorism.

4.4 Preventative measures

arning objectives	**Know** the obligations laid on regulated firms under S18 and S19 (1)(2)(3)(4)(7) Terrorism Act 2000: money laundering of terrorist funds and duty to report; and the Anti-Terrorism, Crime and Security Act 2001, Schedule 2, Part 3 (disclosure of information) and where to find the sanction list for terrorist activities
	Understand the interaction between the rules of FSA, the above legislation and the JMLSG Guidance regarding terrorism

The risk of terrorist funding entering the financial system can be reduced if firms apply satisfactory money laundering strategies and, in particular, know your customer procedures. Firms should assess which countries carry the highest risks and should conduct careful scrutiny of transactions from countries known to be a source of terrorist financing.

In some countries, public information about known or suspected terrorists is available. For example, terrorist names are listed on the US Treasury website.

The **Financial Sanctions Unit** of the Bank of England acts as the agent of the Treasury for the purpose of administering financial sanctions in the UK. **Sanctions lists** are available online within the Publications section of the **Bank of England** web site www.bankofengland.co.uk .

4.5 Duty to report terrorism

A **duty to report** occurs where a person believes or suspects that another person has committed a terrorist offence and where the belief or suspicion has arisen in the course of a trade, profession, business or employment.

An individual commits an offence of failing to report if he does not disclose the suspicion and the information on which it is based to a constable (i.e. the police) as soon as is reasonably practicable.

The following are possible defences to the offence of the failure to report.

- The firm has an established procedure for making disclosures, and the individual properly disclosed the matters in accordance with this procedure.

- The person had a reasonable excuse for not making the disclosure.

A person guilty of failing to report will face a **maximum penalty** of **six months in jail** and/or **£5,000 fine** in the **Magistrates Court** and **five years in jail** and/or an **unlimited fine** in the **Crown Court**.

4.6 Failure to disclose: regulated sector

The Anti-Terrorism, Crime and Security Act 2001 contains additional more onerous legislation applicable to the regulated sector. The definition of the regulated sector is wider than just FSA-authorised firms and includes, for example, bureaux de change.

4.6.1 The offence

Where a person knows or suspects, or has **reasonable grounds** for knowing or suspecting, that another person has committed a terrorist offence and the information came to him in the course of a business in the regulated sector he must report the information to a nominated officer or the police as soon as practicable. Otherwise, that person is committing the offence of failure to disclose.

A nominated officer is the individual in a firm who has been nominated to receive disclosures and is normally the firm's Money Laundering Reporting Officer (MLRO). The disclosure must be made in the course of employment and in accordance with the procedure set out by the firm.

In deciding whether a person has committed an offence under this section of the Anti-Terrorism, Crime and Security Act 2001 a court must consider whether any of the following guidance has been followed.

- Guidance issued by a supervisory authority (e.g. the FSA) or any other appropriate body (e.g. the Investment Management Association 'IMA').

- Guidance approved by the Treasury.

- Whether the guidance was published in such a manner that it is available to persons likely to be affected by it.

4.6.2 The defences

A person has a defence against failure to disclose under this section of the Anti-Terrorism, Crime and Security Act 2001 if he/she has a reasonable excuse for not disclosing the information.

4.6.3 The penalty

A person guilty of failing to disclose will face a **maximum penalty** of **six months in jail** and/or **£5,000 fine** in the **Magistrates Court** and **five years in jail** and/or an **unlimited fine** in the **Crown Court**.

4.7 Protected disclosures

There is clearly a concern that where a disclosure is made in accordance with the above requirements the client may claim this is a breach of client confidentiality. However, the rules state that where disclosures are made in accordance with the reporting rules there will not be a breach of client confidentiality.

5 THE MODEL CODE ON DIRECTORS' DEALINGS

Authority (UKLA), imposes additional regulations on directors of listed companies in the form of the **Model Code**, which appears as an Annex to the Listing Rules.

The purpose of the Model Code is to maintain confidence in the markets by ensuring directors and others with senior management responsibilities are acting in the best interests of the company as a whole and its shareholders. This is as required by directors' fiduciary obligations. The Model Code is not part of the law and breach of the Code does not constitute a criminal offence.

Main provisions of the Model Code affecting directors

- Directors must not deal in securities in their own company nor any contract for difference or other contract designed to make a profit or loss in movements in the price of the company's securities, without seeking **approval** from a senior member of the board, usually the Chairman. If the Chairman or Chief Executive wish to deal, they should seek approval from each other.

- Directors' deals should not be made for the **short term.**

- No trades should be undertaken in the 60 days before publication of the annual report or, if shorter, the period from the end of the financial year up to publication. This is known as a **close period**. The close period before publication of the half-yearly report is from the end of the six-month period up to publication. For quarterly results, the close period is one month prior to the announcement. If, as provided by the **Disclosure and Transparency Rules**, Interim Management Statements are issued instead of quarterly reports, there is no close period and companies must exercise discretion.

5.2 Breaches of the Model Code

A breach of the Model Code will result in disciplinary action being taken by the UKLA. This action may be taken against the individual or the company.

6 DATA PROTECTION AND RECORD KEEPING

earning objective   **Know** the eight Data Protection principles, the need for notification of data controllers with the Information Commissioner; the record-keeping requirements of FSA regulated firms

6.1 Data Protection Act 1998

Under the **Data Protection Act 1998 (DPA 1998)**, where persons process personal data, whether electronically or manually, they must (unless exempt) be registered with the **Information Commissioner** (who maintains a **public registry of data controllers**) and must comply with the DPA provisions. The requirements apply to most organisations and cover all personal data whether it relates to clients, employees, suppliers or any other person. In essence, to comply with DPA 1998, firms should be open with individuals about information held about them and very careful about passing that information to third parties.

6.2 Data Protection Principles

Under DPA 1998, there are **eight Data Protection Principles** (sometimes called the principles of good information handling) with which those controlling personal data must comply.

- **Principle 1** – Personal data shall be **processed fairly and lawfully**. This requires that data shall not be processed unless consent has been obtained from the subject of the data, or the processing is necessary to comply with legal obligations or to protect the vital interests of the subject of the data. Protection of vital interests could be where medical details need to be passed as a result of an accident. Also, where the data is 'sensitive personal data' (e.g. regarding ethnic origin, religion, health, or criminal record) additional requirements are imposed to handle such data.

- **Principle 2** – Personal data shall be obtained only for specified and lawful purposes and shall only be processed in a manner that is compatible with those purposes.

- **Principle 3** – Personal data shall be **adequate, relevant and not excessive** in relation to the purpose or purposes for which they are processed. This is to ensure no more data is held on a person than is strictly required in the circumstances.

- **Principle 4** – Personal data shall be **accurate** and, where necessary, kept up-to-date. This requires reasonable steps to be taken to ensure the accuracy of the data.

- **Principle 5** – Personal data processed for any purpose(s) shall **not be kept for longer** than is necessary for that purpose(s). Data should be reviewed regularly to determine whether it can be deleted.

- **Principle 6** – Personal data shall only be processed in accordance with data subjects, i.e. in accordance with the wishes of those individuals who are the subjects of the data.

- **Principle 7** – Appropriate **technical and organisational measures** shall be taken against unauthorised or unlawful processing of personal data and against accidental loss or destruction of, or damage to, personal data. Consideration should therefore be taken as to those members of staff accessing data and the technology used to store such data.

- **Principle 8** – Personal data shall **not be transferred** to a country or territory outside the **EEA**, unless that country or territory ensures an adequate level of protection of the rights and freedoms of data subjects in relation to the processing of personal data. Guidance as to which countries comply with these requirements can be obtained from the Information Commissioner.

6.3 Breaches of the Principles

Where breaches occur, the **Information Commissioner** has **wide powers** to issue enforcement notices requiring the data controller to take certain action to remedy any breaches.

- Breaches of the DPA 1998 requirements are punishable by a maximum fine of **£5,000** in the **Magistrates' Court** and **unlimited fines** in the **Crown Court**.

- There are also powers to enter premises and seize documents with a court warrant.

6.4 Record keeping: general rules for firms

As a general rule, a firm must arrange for orderly records to be kept of its business and internal organisation, including all of its services and transactions, which must be sufficient to enable the FSA or another competent authority under MiFID to monitor the firm's compliance with the requirements under the regulatory system, and in particular the firm's compliance with all obligations with respect to client.

A firm must retain all records kept by it in relation to its **MiFID business** for a period of **at least five years**.

In relation to its **MiFID business**, a **common platform firm** must retain records in a medium that allows the storage of information in a way accessible, so that the following conditions are met.

BPP
LEARNING MEDIA

- The FSA or any other relevant competent authority under MiFID must be able to access them readily and to reconstitute each key stage of the processing of each transaction

- It must be possible for any corrections or other amendments to be easily ascertained

- It must not be possible for the records otherwise to be manipulated or altered

Records required under the **FSA Handbook** should generally be capable of being reproduced in the **English** language on **paper**, or a firm should be able to provide a translation to English. For business carried on outside the UK, an official language of that country may be used instead.

For **non-MiFID business**, firms should have appropriate security systems and controls. The general principle is that records should be **retained** for **as long as is relevant for the purposes for which they are made**.

6.5 Record keeping and DPA 1998

As a result of DPA 1998, authorised firms should be aware that **records** required to be obtained and kept under FSA rules (including money laundering identification requirements) must also comply with the requirements of DPA 1998.

CHAPTER ROUNDUP

- To act on information not freely available to the market is to commit the criminal offence of insider dealing.

- Various types of behaviour, including insider dealing and manipulation of transactions, can constitute market abuse.

- The FSA's Code of Market Conduct describes behaviours that amount to market abuse, but not exhaustively.

- Money laundering has three stages: placement, layering, integration. Those in the financial services industry must keep alert to possible offences relating to the proceeds of any crime.

- Joint Money Laundering Steering Group guidance emphasises the need for firms to assess risks when implementing money laundering precautions. The 'Know Your Customer' principle implies that firms should, where appropriate, take steps to find out about the customer's circumstances and business.

- It is a criminal offence to assist laundering the proceeds of crime, to fail to report it satisfactorily, or to tip off someone laundering the proceeds of crime.

- The Money Laundering Regulations apply to all authorised firms and individuals. Each firm must have a Nominated Officer, who will decide whether to report suspicions to the Serious Organised Crime Agency.

- Fund raising, use and possession, funding arrangements and money laundering are offences under the Terrorism Act 2000.

- There is a duty to report suspected terrorism to the police.

- The UK Listing Authority imposes additional rules for listed company directors in the Model Code for Directors' Dealings, which should not be undertaken during closed periods or for the short term.

- Those who process personal data must be registered with the Information Commissioner.

- The Data Protection Act 1998 sets out eight Data Protection Principles with which data controllers must comply. The principles are designed to ensure that firms are open with individuals about the information they hold about them, and should be careful about passing it on.

- Under MiFID, the general rule is that firms should keep records for at least five years.

2.	What is the definition of an insider under criminal law?	
3.	What is the maximum penalty for market abuse?	
4.	What are the three stages of money laundering?	■ ■ ■
5.	What legislation makes it a criminal offence for an individual to assist a money launderer?	
6.	What is the maximum penalty for assisting a money launderer?	
7.	Explain what is meant by the 'Nominated Officer' in money laundering prevention provisions.	
8.	What restrictions does the Model Code for Directors Dealings impose?	
9.	Which body maintains a register of data controllers under the Data Protection Act 1998?	

TEST YOUR KNOWLEDGE: ANSWERS

1. The Criminal Justice Act 1993.

   (See Section 1.1)

2. Under CJA 1993, an insider is an individual who knowingly has inside information and knows it is from an inside source.

   (See Section 1.2)

3. An unlimited fine. Other sanctions also include a public statement, an injunction or restitution order.

   (See Section 2.9)

4. Placement, layering and integration.

   (See Section 3.1)

5. The Proceeds of Crime Act 2002.

   (See Section 3.3)

6. Fourteen years in prison and/or an unlimited fine.

   (See Section 3.3.1)

7. The Nominated Officer is someone who has been nominated by their employer to receive reports of suspected money laundering. In practice this will be the Money Laundering Reporting Officer (MLRO) or his deputy.

   (See Section 3.6.3)

8. The Code restricts directors from dealing without permission (normally from the Chairman of the company), dealing for the short-term, i.e. speculating and dealing in the two months, prior to the announcement of interim (six-monthly) or final (annual) results.

   (See Section 5.1)

9. The Information Commissioner.

   (See Section 6.1)

4

INTRODUCTION

The date for implementation of the far-reaching Markets in Financial Instruments Directive (MiFID) is 1 November 2007, and your examination syllabus is based on the regulatory regime following that implementation.

The Financial Services Authority has made substantial revisions to its Handbook to comply with MiFID. To a substantial degree, this has been achieved by 'copying out' MiFID provisions.

There are other earlier European Directives which we also consider in this chapter.

CHAPTER CONTENTS

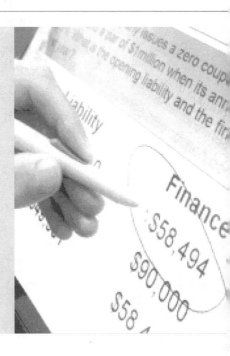

LEARNING OBJECTIVES

Markets in Financial Instruments Directive (MiFID)

- **Know** the purpose and scope of MiFID

  - Passporting within the EEA
  - MiFID v non-MiFID firms
  - Home v host state regulation
  - Investment/ancillary investment services or activities
  - Financial instruments covered by MiFID
  - Exemptions

Capital Requirements Directive (CRD)

- **Know** the purpose of the EU Capital Requirements Directive (CRD)

Electronic Commerce Directive (ECO)

- **Know** the purpose and scope of the Electronic Commerce Directive as it applies to:

  - Domestic ECA providers
  - Incoming ECA providers
  - Outgoing ECA providers

Other EU Directives

- **Know** the purpose and scope of the UCITS Directive (cross-border investment services and permitted investments)

- **Understand** the impact of the Distance Marketing Directive on investment business conducted via non face-to-face methods

- **Know** the purpose and scope of the Prospectus Directive (cross-border prospectuses)

BPP
LEARNING MEDIA

1 MARKETS IN FINANCIAL INSTRUMENTS DIRECTIVE

The **Markets in Financial Instruments Directive (MiFID)** was adopted by the European Council in April 2004 and is part of the European **Financial Services Action Plan**. MiFID was originally due for implementation in April 2006. However, due to the number of changes that MiFID requires the industry to make, the deadline was deferred twice, delaying its effective date until **1 November 2007**.

MiFID replaces the previous Investment Services Directive (ISD), and it applies to all **investment firms**, e.g. investment and retail banks, brokers, assets managers, securities and futures firms, securities issuers and hedge funds. For more detail on the criteria for establishing whether a firm is subject to MiFID, see 'Scope of MiFID', section 1.4 below.

1.2 Implementation of MiFID

The MiFID **Level 1** Directive sets out a number of specific conduct of business 'principles' and a requirement that the European Commission impose more specific 'Level 2' requirements which flesh out the principles.

The MiFID **Level 2** Directive – similar to secondary legislation in the UK – was formally adopted in September 2006 and covers technical implementation measures in the form of **organisational requirements** and **operating conditions**. In addition, the European Commission aims to adopt 'Regulations' which deal with 'market' issues, e.g. transaction reporting and transparency, which will be directly applicable to the UK.

The provisions of the Level 1 and Level 2 Directives are being implemented in the UK through changes to UK law and FSA rules.

New regulation has been required on the basis of **'maximum harmonisation'**, which means that member states should not be able to add rules of their own or make amendments to the original text, a process called **'gold plating'**. The FSA has been accused of 'gold plating' in the past whilst implementing other European Directives.

The European Commission and the Committee of European Securities Regulators (CESR) has been focusing more recently on the delivery of convergent implementation of the MiFID requirements across Member States – this is **Level 3**.

1.3 Passporting within the EEA

The idea of a **'passport'**, which already existed under the ISD, enables firms to use their domestic authorisation to operate not only in their **home state**, but also in other **host states** within the **European Economic Area** (EEA) (EU plus Norway, Iceland and Liechtenstein).

An important aspect of MiFID is that, to make cross-border business easier, the home country principle has been extended. Under MiFID, investment firms which carry out specified investment services and activities (a wider range than under the ISD, as detailed below) are authorised by the member State in which they their registered office is located (the **home state**).

Where a **branch** is set up, **host state** rules will continue to apply. A **tied agent** established in the EEA will be able to act on behalf of a firm instead of the firm needing to set up a branch. (A '**tied agent**', similarly to an **appointed representative** under FSMA 2000, acts on behalf of and under the authority of an investment firm and as a result does not require authorisation.)

Firms which have an **ISD** 'passport' should automatically be given a MiFID passport.

1.4 Scope of MiFID

MiFID applies to a specified range of 'core' **investment services and activities** in relation to specified categories of **financial instruments**, as summarised below.

- **Investment firms** are firms which provide such services or engage in such activities.

- Investment firms are also regulated in respect of various 'non-core' **ancillary services** they may provide (also listed below).

Investment services and activities

- Receiving and transmitting orders
- Execution of orders on behalf of clients
- Dealing on own account
- Managing portfolios on a discretionary basis
- Investment advice
- Underwriting of financial instruments
- Placing of financial instruments
- Operating a Multilateral Trading Facility (MTF)

Financial instruments covered by MiFID

- Transferable securities, e.g. shares and bonds

- Money market instruments

- Units in collective investment undertakings

- Derivatives relating to securities, currencies, interest rates and yields, financial indices and financial measures settled either physically or in cash, including: options, futures, swaps and forward rate agreements

- Commodity derivatives capable of being settled in cash, commodity derivatives capable of being physically settled on a regulated market or multilateral trading facility, and certain other commodity derivatives which are not for commercial purposes

- Derivative instruments for transferring credit risk

- Financial contracts for differences (CFDs)

- Derivatives relating to climatic variables, freight rates, emission allowances, inflation rates or other official economic statistics capable of being settled in cash

Ancillary services

- Safekeeping and administration of financial instruments, including: custodianship; collateral and cash management

- Granting credit or loans to an investor to enable him to carry out a transaction in which the firm is involved

- Advising undertakings on capital structure, industrial strategy

- Advising on mergers and acquisitions

- Foreign exchange services connected with providing investment services

- Investment research, financial analysis or other general recommendations relating to transactions

MiFID's overall scope is narrower than the UK regulatory regime. However, a UK exclusion (in the Regulated Activities Order) will not apply if it conflicts with MiFID.

The **exclusions** are as follows.

- MiFID applies to **EEA-domiciled firms** only. (However, the FSA rules extend MiFID requirements to '**MiFID equivalent activities of third country firms**'.)

- **Credit institutions** (banks and building societies, in the UK) are regulated instead by the Banking Consolidation Directive. However most MiFID provisions will apply to these institutions when they engage in activities within MiFID's scope.

- MiFID does not apply to **insurance companies**.

- MiFID does not apply to **collective investment schemes** nor to their managers, although UCITS managers who provide advice or discretionary management to clients who are not funds will generally be subject to MiFID requirements.

- MiFID **Article 3** allows member states to **exclude** from MiFID the activities of firms whose investment services are limited to receiving and transmitting orders in transferable securities or collective investment schemes, plus related advice. Such firms may not hold client money or securities, nor put themselves in debit to the client. Orders must be transmitted only to investment firms, credit institutions, EEA-regulated collective investment schemes or closed-ended funds traded on a-regulated market in the EEA. Many firms of financial advisers and other retail investment product distributors will meet these criteria, and the UK has enabled them to be excluded from MiFID regulation. Such firms may alternatively opt in, in order to benefit from **passporting**.

1.6 The 'common platform'

The organisational and systems and controls requirements of **MiFID** and the **Capital Requirements Directive (CRD)** are being implemented through a single set of high level rules: this is known as the '**common platform**', since it applies to firms commonly, whichever of the Directives they are subject to.

- Firms subject to both **MiFID and CRD** include most banks and investment firms.

- Firms subject to **MiFID only** are those authorised to provide investment advice and/or receive and transmit orders without having permission to hold client money or securities.

- Firms subject to **CRD only** include banks that do not perform any investment services or other activities within the scope of MiFID.

The implementation of MiFID has led to the introduction of a new **Conduct of Business Sourcebook (COBS),** whose rules are shorter than the previous COB Sourcebook. Various other changes to the FSA Handbook have also been necessary.

1.7 Multilateral Trading Facilities and Systematic Internalisers

MiFID introduces the ability to passport **Multilateral Trading Facilities (MTFs)** as a 'core' investment service. MTFs are systems where firms provide services similar to those of exchanges by matching client orders. A firm taking proprietary positions with a client is not running an MTF. There has been debate about the requirements to be imposed on MTFs. The Committee of European Securities Regulators (CESR) has published standards they expect to be met by MTFs, including notifying the home state regulator of activities, fair and orderly trading, price transparency, clarity of systems and reduction of financial crime.

A **Systematic Internaliser** is an investment firm which deals on its own account by executing client orders outside a regulated market or a MTF. MiFID will require such firms to publish firm quotes in liquid shares (for orders below 'standard market size') and to maintain those quotes on a regular and continuous basis during normal business hours.

2   CAPITAL REQUIREMENTS DIRECTIVE

Learning objective   **Know** the purpose of the EU Capital Requirements Directive (CRD)

2.1 Introduction

The overall aim of capital requirements rules is to ensure that firms remain solvent by having greater assets at their command than they will need to cover their positions. In general, a firm must maintain, at all times, financial resources in excess of its financial resources requirement.

As a result of the implementation of the Capital Adequacy Directive (CAD), the FSA rules have incorporated two distinct sets of rules relating to capital adequacy, found in the **Interim Prudential Sourcebook (IPRU)** of the FSA Handbook.

Before 1 January 2007, the **Interim Prudential Sourcebook for Investment Businesses (IPRU (INV))** was the part of the Handbook that dealt with capital requirements for investment firms subject to the position risk requirements of the previous version of the Capital Adequacy Directive. Now, however, investment firms which are subject to the risk-based capital requirements of the Capital Adequacy Directive are subject to the **General Prudential sourcebook (GENPRU)** and the **Prudential sourcebook for Banks, Building Societies and Investment Firms (BIPRU)**.

2.2 Basel II and the Capital Requirements Directive

The UK financial resources requirements are based on the Basel Capital Accord known as '**Basel II**'. Basel II is implemented in the European Union via the **Capital Requirements Directive (CRD)** for credit institutions and investment firms. It directly affects banks, building societies and certain types of investment firm in the UK. CRD amends the two existing directives: the **Capital Adequacy Directive (CAD)** and the **Banking Consolidation Directive (BCD)**.

The **Basel Committee on Banking Supervision** does not have legal powers but creates common standards and guidelines of best practice with the aim that individual states will implement these in their own law. The Committee has tried to reduce divergences in international supervisory standards. They seek to ensure that all foreign banking establishments are actually supervised by someone and that supervision is adequate.

The revised Basel Capital Accord, referred to as Basel II (the full formal title is *International convergence of capital measurement and capital standards - a revised framework*), is reflected in EU law via the **Capital Requirements Directive** whose implementation date was 1 January 2007.

2.2.1 Key aspects of Basel II

Basel II is a revision of the existing prudential framework and aims to make the framework more risk-sensitive and more representative of modern banks' risk management practices. The new framework aims to leave the overall level of capital held by banks collectively broadly unchanged.

The **capital adequacy framework** is intended to reduce the probability of consumer loss or market disruption as a result of prudential failure. It does so by seeking to ensure that the financial resources held by a firm are commensurate with the risks associated with the business profile and the control environment within the firm.

2.2.2 The three pillars

The framework consists of three '**pillars**'.

- **Pillar 1** sets out the minimum capital requirements firms will be required to meet for credit, market and operational risk. There is a two-stage process to determine a firm's minimum capital requirement reflecting market, credit and operational risk. The first stage involves assessing the category of the firm. The second stage is to establish the method for calculating the minimum capital requirement.

- **Pillar 2:** firms and FSA supervisors have to take a view on whether a firm should hold additional capital against risks not covered in Pillar 1 and must take action accordingly. Under Pillar 2 a firm will, amongst other things, have to assess regularly the amount of internal capital it considers adequate to cover all of the risks to which it is exposed within the context of its overall risk management framework. BIPRU provides guidance on some of those risks.

- **Pillar 3** aims to improve market discipline by requiring firms to publish certain details of their risks, capital and risk management. This is intended to allow market participants to assess key pieces of information on a firm's capital, risk exposures and risk assessment processes.

3 ELECTRONIC COMMERCE DIRECTIVE

earning objective **Know** the purpose and scope of the Electronic Commerce Directive as it applies to: domestic ECA providers, incoming ECA providers and outgoing ECA providers

3.1 Purpose and scope

The Electronic Commerce Directive has been implemented in the UK and aims to provide freedom for EEA firms to carry out Electronic Commerce Activity (ECA) freely into other EEA states. The Directive simplified previous rules so that an EEA firm doing ECA generally only has to comply with its **home state** conduct of business rules, therefore introducing a **country of origin** approach to regulation.

Electronic Commerce Activity (ECA) is defined as any electronic financial service which would be a regulated activity if it were provided by non-electronic means, e.g. the provision of electronic broking services.

The rules apply to three types of ECA provider:

- Incoming
- Outgoing
- Domestic

3.2 Incoming ECA providers

An **incoming ECA provider** is an EEA firm (other than a UK firm) carrying out ECA with or for a UK consumer. This would, for example, cover a French firm providing ECA to a UK consumer.

An incoming ECA provider has to comply with the applicable laws in the country of origin (home state) from which the service is provided, e.g. France, and not FSMA 2000 or the FSA Handbook.

This makes it easier for firms to provide cross-border services, but the general rule is subject to certain derogations. These derogations would allow the host State, in our example the UK, to impose certain 'host State' (i.e. UK) requirements. These derogations are allowed as the host state has continuing responsibility for consumer protection and include requirements to provide basic terms and conditions in English. Therefore subject to certain derogations set out in FSA regulations, the FSA Handbook and FSMA 2000 do not apply to incoming ECA providers.

3.3 Outgoing ECA providers

An **outgoing ECA provider** is one which carries on electronic commerce activity with an EEA recipient (other than a UK recipient) from a UK establishment, whether or not the recipient is a consumer. This would, for example, cover a UK firm providing ECA to a French consumer.

There are minimum information requirements on outgoing ECA providers such as information about the firm. These requirements are in addition to the requirements otherwise applicable to firms when they carry on regulated activities in the UK as set out in FSMA 2000 and the FSA Handbook, e.g. conduct of business rules.

The electronic commerce rules relate to all regulated firms in relation to a financial promotion which is an outgoing electronic commerce communication. An outgoing electronic commerce communication is one which is made from an establishment in the United Kingdom to a person in an EEA State (other than the UK). This would, for example, cover a UK firm marketing their services to a French consumer. The rules require the firm to comply with Chapter 4 of the Conduct of Business (COB) rules on financial promotions as if the person to whom the communication is made or directed was in the UK.

3.4 Domestic ECA providers

From the UK perspective, a **domestic ECA provider** is an FSA-authorised firm which provides ECA from an establishment which it has in the United Kingdom, with or for a UK recipient or a recipient outside the EEA. This would, for example, cover a UK firm providing ECA to a UK or a Canadian consumer.

In the first scenario, not surprisingly, UK rules apply to the relationship. In the second scenario, the UK firm would have to comply with Canadian rules as the recipient is not in the EEA. So the rules revert to a 'host State' position. However, as well as considering the host state rules, the UK firm is required to supply certain minimum information requirements to the ECA recipient regardless of the recipient's location.

4 OTHER EU DIRECTIVES

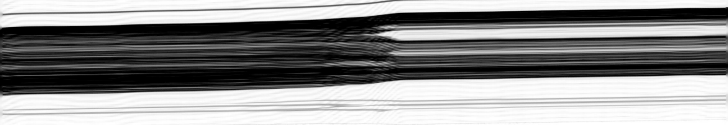

The EU has enacted a number of directives relevant to collective investment schemes. These are known as the **UCITS Directives**. **UCITS** stands for **Undertakings for Collective Investment in Transferable Securities**.

The aim of UCITS was to create a type of passport throughout the EEA for collective investment schemes that meet the UCITS criteria. The idea was to promote the free movement of services in the same way as the ISD allows investment firms to passport their services throughout the EEA.

The CIS must be authorised in its home State and receive confirmation from its home State regulator that the CIS complies with UCITS criteria. That confirmation is then provided to the host State regulator, who the fund manager notifies that they wish to market the fund in that EEA state. Although UCITS aims to make cross-border sales of CIS easier, the CIS must comply with the marketing rules of the host state and the documentation requirements of the directive.

The first **UCITS Directive** contained a number of limitations. The main limitation was that the definition of **permitted investments** was very narrow. This meant that generally schemes wanting to use UCITS to sell cross-border could only invest in transferable securities. Initially the permitted investments included securities funds (containing for example shares and bonds), warrant funds and umbrella funds, where each sub-fund is either a securities fund or a warrant fund. In addition, the first UCITS Directive contained various categories of scheme, e.g. a securities fund and an umbrella fund, with separate investment rules for each category.

UCITS was updated in 2002 by the **UCITS III Product Directive,** which expanded the range of assets which UCITS funds are able to invest in. It also made provision for a single UCITS scheme to replace all of the previous categories of fund which had separate rules.

4.1.2 UCITS schemes

As a result of the **UCITS Product Directive**, UCITS schemes are now able to invest in the following types of **permitted investment**.

- Transferable securities (see below)
- Money market instruments
- Forward contracts and financial derivatives
- Deposits
- Units in other Collective Investment Schemes

Transferable securities comprise shares, instruments creating or acknowledging indebtedness (e.g. debentures, loan stock, bonds, government and public securities) and certificates representing certain securities. car.

Although **commodity derivatives** are excluded, it would appear that derivatives based on commodity indices could be eligible as financial derivatives.

| Exam tip | A common exam question is about commodity derivatives being outside the scope of UCITS schemes. |

4.1.3 UCITS and non-UCITS schemes

Under FSA Handbook (COLL) rules, both UCITS and non-UCITS retail schemes can invest in a variety of types of instrument, including warrants and financial derivatives, within their overall investment objectives, provided that they apply a risk management procedure. A non-UCITS retail scheme can invest in an even wider range of assets, including gold or 100% investment in immovable property.

Non-UCITS schemes may also **borrow** up to 10% of the fund value on a **permanent** basis, while UCITS retail schemes are only permitted to borrow on a **temporary** basis, again to 10% of the fund value.

4.2 Distance Marketing Directive and Distance Marketing Regulations

Learning objective	Understand the impact of the Distance Marketing Directive on investment business conducted via non face-to-face methods

The EU **Distance Marketing Directive (DMD)** covers the distance marketing of financial services. This Directive has been enacted in the UK via the **Financial Services (Distance Marketing) Regulations 2004**.

COBS Chapter 5 on *The distance marketing disclosure rules* includes provisions conforming to the DMD. COBS clarifies how the **Distance Marketing Directive (DMD)** and the Distance Marketing Regulations should be interpreted by authorised firms. It requires that certain product disclosures are given to **consumers** who conclude contracts at a distance.

The FSA has taken the view that responsibility for the DMD requirements applies to the Home State except in the case of a branch, in which case responsibility rests with the EEA State in which the branch is located. This means that the relevant COBS rules will apply to branches in the UK, including branches of foreign (EEA or non-EEA) firms.

4.2.1 Disclosure requirements

The DMD introduced requirements to provide consumers with certain **detailed information** before a contract is concluded, including information about:

- The identity of the supplier (including geographical address)
- Product details (including price and fees), and
- Particulars of the contract (including rights of cancellation)

During **voice telephony** communications, only specified abbreviated distance marketing information needs to be provided. However, the standard distance marketing information must still be provided on a durable medium in good time before the customer is bound by any distance contract or offer.

4.2.2 Consumer

The DMD provides protections for any individual who is a **consumer**, meaning a natural person (i.e. an individual) who concludes a **distance contract** outside of their trade, business or profession.

The Directive covers individuals acting, for example:

- As personal representatives, including executors, unless they are acting in a professional capacity, e.g. a solicitor acting as executor, or
- In personal or other family circumstances for example, as trustee of a family trust

but excludes individuals acting, for example:

- As trustee of a trust, such as a housing or NHS trust, or

- As member of the governing body of a club or other unincorporated association, such as a trade body or a student union, or

- As a pension trustee

internet.

The following factors help determine whether a contract is concluded under an '**organised distance sales or service-provision scheme**'.

- There must have been no '**simultaneous physical presence**' of the firm and the **consumer** throughout the offer, negotiation and conclusion of the contract. So, for example, contracts offered, negotiated and concluded over the internet, through a telemarketing operation or by post will normally be **distance contracts**. A **consumer** may visit the local office of the firm in the course of the offer, negotiation or conclusion of the contract with that firm. Wherever, in the literal sense, there has been 'simultaneous physical presence' of the firm and the **consumer** at the time of such a visit, any ensuing contract will **not** be a **distance contract**.

- Services provided on a strictly occasional basis and outside a commercial structure dedicated to the conclusion of **distance contracts** are not governed by the DMD.

- A one-off transaction effected exclusively by distance means to meet an emergency will not be a **distance contract**.

- If a firm normally operates face-to-face and has no facilities in place enabling a **consumer** to deal with it customarily by distance means, the DMD will not apply.

4.2.4 Initial service agreement and successive operations

A firm's contract with a customer may take the form of an **initial service agreement** followed by a **series of separate operations** over time. Where this is the case, the DMD disclosure and cancellation requirements apply in relation to the initial service agreement only and not to the successive or separate operations.

However, if new elements are added to the **initial service agreement**, the addition of those new elements is treated as a new contract, to which the DMD disclosure and cancellation requirements apply. For example, the opening of a bank account would be a initial service agreement, the deposit or withdrawal of funds from that account would be a successive or series of separate operations, but adding a debit card to the account constitutes a new element to which the DMD disclosure and cancellation requirements apply.

Other examples of **initial service agreements** and **successive operations** are as follows.

- Opening a brokerage account for the purposes of trading securities, and transactions under that account

- Establishing a facility to enable a customer to subscribe to an ISA for the present and future tax years, and successive subscriptions under that agreement

- Subscribing to an investment trust savings scheme, and successive purchases or sales of shares under that scheme

- Concluding a life policy, pension contract or stakeholder pension scheme that includes a pre-selected option providing for future increases or decreases in regular premiums or payments, and subsequent index-linked changes to those premiums or increases or decreases to pension contributions following fluctuations in salary

93

The DMD disclosure requirements will not apply to **successive operations** of the same nature over time, e.g. the subscription of units into the same Collective Investment Scheme provided there has been an operation of the same nature within the past year. If there has been a break of longer than a year, the next operation will be treated as the first in a new series of operations and the DMD disclosure requirements will apply.

4.2.5 Use of intermediaries

The mere fact that an intermediary (acting for the firm or for the **consumer**) is involved does not make the sale of a financial product or service a **distance contract**.

4.2.6 Distance contracts for intermediation services

In a small number of cases, intermediaries will themselves fall within the scope of DMD, e.g. where the intermediary agrees to provide continuing advisory, broking or portfolio management services for a **consumer**.

However, the DMD is only relevant if:

- There is a contract between the intermediary and the consumer in respect of the intermediary's mediation services, and

- The contract is a distance contract, and

- The contract is concluded other than merely as a stage in the provision of another service by the intermediary or another person

4.3 The Prospectus Directive and cross-border prospectuses

Learning objective | **Know** the purpose and scope of the Prospectus Directive (cross-border prospectuses)

The **Prospectus Directive** is an EU directive which came into force in December 2003. It was implemented in the UK with effect from 1 July 2005 by the Prospectus Regulations 2005, which amended Part IV FSMA 2000, and by the Prospectus Rules in the FSA Handbook.

The Directive requires that a prospectus is produced whenever there is a public offer of securities or where securities are admitted to trading on a regulated market. The Directive specifies the content of prospectuses and requires that they are approved by the relevant **competent authority** – in the UK, this is the **FSA**.

These requirements are designed to increase protection of investors by ensuring the quality of prospectuses and to enhance international market efficiency through the issue of single approved prospectuses for use throughout the EEA.

The Directive identifies two types of situation where prospectuses are required:

- An offer of securities to the general public
- Admission of securities to trading on a regulated market

Under the Prospectus Directive, there is a **'single passport'** for issuers, with the result that a prospectus approved by one competent authority can be used across the EEA without any further approval or burdensome administrative procedures in other member states. If the competent authority in the relevant member state approves the prospectus, it will be accepted throughout the EEA.

A prospectus is required on admission of a company's transferable securities to a **regulated market** in the EEA: the London Stock Exchange is such a regulated market.

London's **Alternative Investment Market (AIM)** was deregulated in October 2004, and there are some exemptions which may apply to AIM IPOs (Initial Public Offers), takeovers and fund raising.

The overall position is that a prospectus is required in the case of an offer of transferable securities to the public in the EEA, unless an exemption applies. An 'offer' is defined broadly and covers any communication in any form and by any means which presents sufficient information about the terms of the offer and the securities offered such as to enable an investor to decide to buy or subscribe to those securities.

The main **exemptions** are as follows.

- Offers made only to qualified investors, which includes regulated institutions and investment companies, as well as some UK-resident persons and small and medium-sized enterprises who meet specified criteria and are registered as qualified investors with the FSA

- Cases where the total consideration for the offer over a 12-month period is less than €2,900,000

- Offers made to fewer than 100 persons per EEA state other than qualified investors

- Documents where securities are offered in connection with a takeover or merger, if they contain information similar to that in a prospectus: such documents will not require formal approval

CHAPTER ROUNDUP

- The Markets in Financial Instruments Directive (MiFID) replaces the Investment Services Directive (ISD), with effect from 1 November 2007.

- MiFID applies to all 'investment firms', including investment banks, securities dealers and portfolio managers.

- Under MiFID, firms which carry out specified investment services and activities (a wider range than under the ISD) are authorised by the member state in which they their registered office is located. Where a branch is set up, host state rules will continue to apply. 'Passporting' enables them to operate throughout the EEA.

- MiFID investment firms are also regulated in respect of various ancillary services they may provide.

- The MiFID regime does not apply to credit institutions, which are regulated by the Banking Consolidation Directive. Nor does it apply to insurance companies or collective investment schemes. Many firms of financial advisers are also excluded if they do not hold client money. Such firms may 'opt in', to take advantage of passporting.

- The Capital Requirements Directive seeks to ensure that firms remain solvent and are able to cover their positions at all times.

- An EEA firm engaged in electronic commerce is generally only required to comply with its home state conduct of business rules.

- UCITS Directives enable passporting for collective investment schemes which meet UCITS criteria, in the interests of facilitating cross-border financial services within Europe. The scheme must be regulated or authorised in its home state, and the home state regulator will confirm that the scheme complies with UCITS criteria.

- Distance marketing rules, which follow the Distance Marketing Directive, require consumers to be provided with specified information before a distance contract is concluded.

- In the interests of investor protection, the Prospectus Directive imposes disclosure standards when there is an offer of securities. A Prospectus which is formally approved in one EEA member state can be used across the EEA without further approval: this is referred to as the 'single passport' for issuers.

TEST YOUR KNOWLEDGE

Check your knowledge of the chapter here, without referring back to the text.

1.	What is meant by 'gold plating'?	
2.	Outline how 'home state' and 'host state' rules apply under MiFID.	
3.	Which of the following financial instruments are normally covered by MiFID: (a) Cocoa futures (b) Contracts for differences (c) Forward rate agreements?	▪ ▪ ▪
4.	To which of the following does MiFID normally apply: (a) Portfolio managers; (b) Insurance companies; (c) Collective investment schemes?	▪ ▪ ▪
5.	What is the significance of 'ancillary services' within the MiFID framework?	
6.	What is the overall purpose of capital requirements rules?	
7.	Outline the central purpose of the Electronic Commerce Directive.	
8.	What does 'UCITS' mean?	
9.	Outline the main effect of the Distance Marketing Directive.	
10.	What is the effect of the 'single passport' under the Prospectus Directive?	

TEST YOUR KNOWLEDGE: ANSWERS

1. 'Gold plating' refers to the process of adding further rules when implementing a Directive.

   (See Section 1.2)

2. Under MiFID, investment firms are authorised by the member state in which their registered office is located and home state rules will apply. Where a branch is set up, host state rules will however apply.

   (See Section 1.3)

3. All of these instruments are covered by MiFID. Cocoa futures are a type of commodity derivative.

   (See Section 1.4)

4. MiFID applies to portfolio managers, but insurance companies and collective investment schemes are covered by exclusions.

   (See Sections 1.4 and 1.5)

5. MiFID regulated firms are also regulated in respect of ancillary services they provide.

   (See Section 1.4)

6. Capital requirements rules seek to ensure that firms remain solvent by having greater assets at their command than they will need to cover their positions. In general, a firm must maintain, at all times, financial resources in excess of its financial resources requirement.

   (See Section 2.1)

7. The Directive has the result that an EEA firm carrying out electronic commerce activity generally only has to comply with its home state conduct of business rules, therefore following a country of origin approach to regulation.

   (See Section 3.1)

8. UCITS stands for 'Undertakings for Collective Investment in Transferable Securities'.

   (See Section 4.1)

9. The Directive requires that certain product disclosures are given to consumers who conclude contracts at a distance.

   (See Section 4.2)

10. The 'single passport' concept means that a prospectus approved by one competent authority can be used across the EEA without any further approval or burdensome administrative procedures in other member states.

    (See Section 4.3)

5

FSA Conduct of Business and Client Assets Sourcebooks

INTRODUCTION

The FSA Principles for Businesses are central to the 'principles-based' approach to regulation. Recall that protection of consumers is one of the FSA's four statutory objectives. The FSA has made detailed rules in the 'Conduct of Business Sourcebook' (COBS) which are aimed largely at providing such protection.

The COBS rules cover a wide range of operational areas, and have been substantially revised in 2007 following the implementation of the Markets in Financial Instruments Directive (MiFID). This underlines the fact that regulation is increasingly being determined at the European level.

LEARNING OBJECTIVES

The application and general provisions of the FSA Conduct of Business Sourcebook

- **Know** the firms subject to the FSA Conduct of Business Sourcebook

- **Know** the activities which are subject to the FSA Conduct of Business Sourcebook including Eligible Counterparty Business and transactions between regulated market participants

- **Know** the impact of location on firms/activities of the application of the FSA Conduct of Business Sourcebook: permanent place of business in UK

- **Know** how the application of the FSA Conduct of Business Sourcebook applies to appointed representatives

- **Know** the provisions of the FSA Conduct of Business Sourcebook regarding electronic media (Glossary definitions of 'Durable Medium' and 'Website Conditions')

Accepting clients

- **Understand** client status
    - The application of the rules on client classification
    - Definition of client
    - Retail client, professional client and eligible counterparty
    - When a person is acting as agent for another person
    - The rule on classifying elective professional clients
    - The rule on elective eligible counterparties
    - Providing clients with a higher level of protection
    - The requirement to provide notifications of client categorisation

- **Know** the requirement for firms to provide client agreements, when a client agreement is required to be signed and when it is acceptable to be provided to clients

- **Know** the requirement to provide information to clients prior to providing services to clients including information relating to the nature and risk of the services and designated investments being offered

- **Know** the rules on the provision of information in connection with the services of managing investments

- **Know** the rules on the provision of information concerning safeguarding of designated investments belonging to clients and client money

- **Know** the rules on disclosure of costs and associated charges, timing of disclosure, medium of disclosure, changes to information provided to the client and compensation information

- **Know** the rules on disclosure of information regarding packaged products

- **Know** the rules, guidance and evidential provisions regarding reliance on others

Communicating with clients, including financial promotions

- **Know** the application of the rules on co~
firms' responsibilities for a~

- **Know** th~

- **Know** the main exceptions to the financial promotions rules in COBS (and the glossary definition of 'excluded communications'), the limitations in connection to MiFID business and the existence of the Financial Promotions Order

- **Know** the types and methods of communication addressed by COBS 4

- **Know** the rules on prospectus advertisements

- **Know** the general rule in connection with communicating with retail clients

- **Know** the rules on past, simulated past and future performance

- **Know** the rule on financial promotions containing offers or invitations

- **Know** the rules on unwritten promotions and the restriction on cold calling

- **Know** the rule on financial promotions for overseas persons

- **Know** the requirement for approving financial promotions and the circumstances of relying on another firm's confirmation of compliance

Advising and selling

- **Understand** the application of the rules on identifying client needs and advising

- **Understand** the purpose of the suitability rules and the requirement for assessing suitability

- **Understand** the information which a firm must obtain from a client in order to make a suitability assessment, and the guidance on assessing suitability

- **Know** the application of the assessing suitability rules for professional clients

- **Understand** the obligation to provide a retail client with a suitability report

- **Know** the timing and contents of a suitability report

- **Know** the application and purpose of the rules on advising on packaged products, including the scope and range of advising

- **Understand** the application and purpose of the rules on non-advised sales

- **Understand** the obligations for assessing appropriateness

- **Know** the obligation to warn the client

- **Know** the circumstances in which it is not necessary to assess appropriateness

Product disclosure and the customer's right to cancel

- **Know** the purpose of the rule on the sale of packaged products to retail clients, the rule requiring the provision of key features to retail clients and the main features to be explained in the key features

- **Know** the purpose and requirements of the cancellation and withdrawal rights

Dealing and managing

- **Know** the application of the rules on dealing and managing

- **Understand** the application and purpose of the principles and rules on conflict of interest; the rules on identifying conflicts and types of conflicts; the rules on recording and managing conflicts; and the rule on disclosure of conflicts

- **Know** the rule requiring a conflicts policy and the contents of the policy

- **Understand** the rules on Chinese walls

- **Understand** the rules on managing conflicts in connection with investment research and research recommendations

- **Know** the application and purpose of the rule on prohibition of inducements and the use of dealing commission, including what benefits can be supplied/obtained under such agreements

- **Understand** the requirements of providing best execution

- **Understand** the requirements for an order execution policy, its disclosure, the requirements for consent and review

- **Understand** the rules on following specific instructions from a client

- **Understand** the rules on monitoring the effectiveness of execution arrangements and policy; demonstrating compliance with the execution policy; and the duties of portfolio managers and receivers and transmitters to act in a client's best interest

- **Understand** the rule on client order handling and the conditions to be satisfied when carrying out client orders

- **Understand** the rules on aggregation and allocation of orders and the rules on aggregation and allocation of transactions for own account

- **Know** the rules on client limit orders – the obligation to make unexecuted client limit orders public

- **Understand** the application and purpose of the personal account dealing rule and the restrictions on personal account dealing

- **Know** the arrangements required to comply with the personal account dealing rules including the notification requirements, and exceptions regarding personal account dealing

- **Understand** the guidance on churning and switching

Reporting to clients

- **Know** the requirement to report to your client including confirmation of transactions and periodic statements

Client assets

- **Understand** the purpose of the client money and custody rules in CASS, including the requirement for segregation and that it is held in trust

- **Know** the requirements for reconciling client assets and client money including the timing and identification of discrepancies

- **Know** the exemptions from the requirements of the CASS rules

1 COBS: APPLICATION AND GENERAL PROVISIONS

Know the firms subject to the FSA Conduct of Business Sourcebook

Know the activities which are subject to the FSA Conduct of Business Sourcebook including Eligible Counterparty Business and transactions between regulated market participants

Know the impact of location on firms/activities of the application of the FSA Conduct of Business Sourcebook: permanent place of business in UK

Know how the application of the FSA Conduct of Business Sourcebook applies to appointed representatives

1.1 COBS

The FSA includes various rules in a large section of its Handbook called the **Conduct of Business Sourcebook**. The Conduct of Business Rules have been revised extensively, and shortened, with the implementation of the Markets in Financial Instruments Directive (MiFID), with effect from November 2007. The new Sourcebook has sometimes been referred to as 'NEWCOB', but is now referred to by the abbreviation '**COBS**'. (The version which COBS replaced had the abbreviation 'COB'.)

1.2 General application rule

The **general application rule** is that **COBS** applies to an authorised **firm** in respect of the following activities when carried out from one of its (or its **appointed representative's**) **UK** establishments.

- Accepting deposits
- Designated investment business
- Long-term life insurance business

Many rules (except the financial promotion rules) only apply when the firm is doing **designated investment business** with customers.

The term '**designated investment business**' has a narrower meaning than the concept of '**regulated activities**' by excluding activities relating to Lloyd's business, deposits, funeral plans, mortgages, pure protection policies and general insurance contracts. Following the implementation of MiFID, operating a **multilateral trading facility (MTF)** is designated investment business.

There are **modifications** to the general application rule. Only some of the COBS rules apply to **eligible counterparty business** which is MiFID or equivalent third country (that is, **non-EEA**) business. The term 'eligible counterparty' is explained later in this chapter. The following COBS rules **do not** apply to such business.

- Conduct of business obligations, except 'Agent as client' and 'Reliance on others' rules
- Communicating with clients (including financial promotions rules)
- Rules on information about the firm and its services
- Client agreements
- Appropriateness rules (for non-advised sales)
- Best execution, client order handling and use of dealing commission
- Information about designated investments
- Reporting information to clients

1.3 Further general provisions

The **territorial scope** of COBS is modified to ensure compatibility with European law: this is called the **'EEA territorial scope rule'**. One of the effects of the EEA territorial scope rule is to override the application of COBS to the overseas establishments of EEA firms in a number of cases, including circumstances covered by MiFID, the Distance Marketing Directive or the Electronic Commerce Directive. In some circumstances, the rules on financial promotions and other communications will apply to communications made by UK firms to persons located outside the United Kingdom and will not apply to communications made to persons inside the United Kingdom by EEA firms.

For a UK **MiFID investment firm**, COBS rules within the scope of MiFID generally apply to its MiFID business carried on from a **UK branch or establishment**. COBS also applies to EEA MiFID investment firms carrying out business from a UK establishment. However, certain provisions (on investment research, non-independent research and on personal transactions) apply on a **'Home State' basis**: those rules will apply to all establishments in the EEA for the UK firm, and will not apply to a non-UK EEA firm.

COBS provisions on **client limit orders** do not apply to transactions between the operator of a MTF and its members, for MiFID or equivalent third country business. Members or participants in a **regulated market** do not have to apply client limit orders rules to each other, again for MiFID or equivalent third country business. However, in both cases, these rules must be applied if the members are executing orders on behalf of **clients**.

1.4 Communications by electronic media

Learning objective	**Know** the provisions of the FSA Conduct of Business Sourcebook regarding electronic media (Glossary definitions of 'Durable Medium' and 'Website Conditions')

Where a rule requires a notice to be delivered in writing, a firm may comply using **electronic media**. The COBS rules often specify that communication must be in a **durable medium**.

Durable medium means:

- Paper, or

- Any instrument (e.g. an email message) which enables the recipient to store information addressed personally to him in a way accessible for future reference for a period of time adequate for the purposes of the information and which allows the unchanged reproduction of the information stored. This will include the recipient's computer hard drive or other storage devices on which the electronic mail is stored, but not internet websites unless they fulfil the criteria in this definition.

Some communications are allowed to be delivered either in a durable medium or via a website, where the **website conditions** are satisfied.

The **website conditions** are specified as follows:

(1)   The provision of the information in that medium must be appropriate to the context in which the business between the firm and the client is, or is to be, carried on (i.e. there is evidence that the client has regular access to the internet, such as the provision by the client of an e-mail address).

(2)   The client must specifically consent to the provision of that information in that form.

(3)   The client must be notified electronically of the address of the website, and the place on the website where the information may be accessed.

(4)   The information must be up-to-date.

(5)   The information must be accessible continuously by means of that website for such period of time as the client may reasonably need to inspect it.

2 CLIENT CATEGORISATION

earning objective **Understand** client status: The application of the rules on client classification; Definition of client; Retail client, professional client and eligible counterparty; When a person is acting as agent for another person; The rule on classifying elective professional clients; The rule on elective eligible counterparties; Providing clients with a higher level of protection; The requirement to provide notifications of client categorisation

2.1 Levels of protection

Within any cost-effective regulatory system, protection provided ought to be **proportionate** to the need for protection. This is because there is not only a cost element to protection but also an inverse relationship with freedom. It is desirable that those who do not require high protection are given more freedom to trade without the restrictions that the rules inevitably bring.

The **size** and **financial awareness** of **clients** will determine the level of protection. As the size/knowledge increases, protection will decrease. A system of categorising clients can help determine that the level of protection is appropriate to the client.

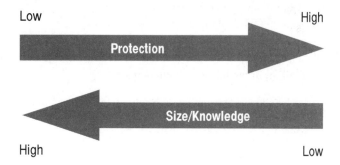

While this would ideally be a continuous process, gradually moving from full protection to no protection, in practical terms this is an impossibility.

2.2 Client categories

The terms used to classify clients has changed following the implementation of **MiFID** and the introduction of the new COBS.

Firms (unless they are providing only the special level of **basic advice** on a **stakeholder product**) are obliged to classify all clients who are undertaking **designated investment business,** before doing such business.

MiFID creates three client categories:

- **Eligible counterparties** – who are either **per se** or **elective** eligible counterparties
- **Professional clients** – who are either **per se** or **elective** professional clients
- **Retail clients**

As well as setting up criteria to classify clients into these categories, MiFID provides for clients to **change** their initial classification, on request.

2.2.1 Clients

A **client** is a person to whom an authorised **firm** provides a service in the course of carrying on a **regulated activity** or, in the case of MiFID or equivalent third country business, a person to whom a firm provides an **ancillary service**.

2.2.2 Retail clients

Retail clients are defined as those clients who are not professional clients or eligible counterparties.

2.2.3 Professional clients

Some undertakings are automatically recognised as **professional clients**. Accordingly, these entities may be referred to as *per se* professional clients. (An **undertaking** is a company, partnership or unincorporated association.)

Clients who are *per se* **professional clients** are as follows.

- Entities that **require authorisation or regulation** to operate in the financial markets, including: credit institutions, investment firms, other financial institutions, insurance companies, collective investment schemes and pension funds and their management companies, commodity and commodity derivatives dealers, 'local' derivatives dealing firms, and other institutional investors

- In relation to **MiFID** or equivalent third country business, a **large undertaking** – meaning one that meets two of the following size requirements:

  - €20,000,000 Balance sheet total
  - €40,000,000 Net turnover
  - €2,000,000 Own funds

- In relation to business that is not **MiFID** or equivalent third country business, a **large undertaking** meeting **either** of the following requirements:

  (a) Called up share capital of at least £10,000,000 or equivalent, or

  (b) Two of the three following size tests:

    - €12,500,000 balance sheet total
    - €25,000,000 net turnover
    - 250 average number of employees in the year

- Central banks, international institutions, and national and regional government bodies

- Institutional investors whose main activity is to invest in financial instruments

A firm may treat a retail client as an **elective professional client** if the following tests are met.

- **Qualitative test.** The firm assesses adequately the client's **expertise**, **experience** and **knowledge** and thereby gains reasonable assurance that, for the transactions or services envisaged, the client is capable of making his own investment decisions and understanding the risks involved.

- **Quantitative test.** In the case of **MiFID** or equivalent third country business, at least **two** of the following three criteria must apply:

  - The client has carried out at least ten 'significant' transactions per quarter on the relevant market, over the last four quarters

  - The client's portfolio, including cash deposits, exceeds €500,000

  - The client has knowledge of the transactions envisaged from at least one year's professional work in the financial sector

Additionally, for professional client status to apply:

- The client must agree in writing to be treated as a professional client

- The firm must give written warning of the protections and compensation rights which may be lost

- The client must state in writing, separately from the contract, that it is aware of the consequences of losing protections

It is the responsibility of the professional client to keep the firm informed about changes (e.g. in portfolio size or company size) which could affect their categorisation.

COBS states that an elective professional client should not be presumed to have market knowledge and experience comparable to a *per se* professional client.

2.2.4 Eligible counterparties

In relation to MiFID or equivalent third country business, a client can only be an eligible counterparty in relation to eligible counterparty business.

The following, and their non-EEA equivalents, are *per se* **eligible counterparties** (i.e. they are automatically recognised as eligible counterparties).

- Investment firms
- Credit institutions
- Insurance companies
- UCITS collective investment schemes, and their management companies
- Pension funds, and their management companies
- Other financial institutions authorised or regulated under the law of the EU or an EEA state
- Certain own-account commodity derivatives dealers and 'local' derivatives firms
- National governments
- Central banks
- Supranational organisations

A firm may treat an undertaking as an **elective eligible counterparty** if the client:

- Is a *per se* professional client (unless it is such by virtue of being an institutional investor), or

- Is an elective professional client and requests the categorisation, but only in respect of the transactions and services for which it counts as a professional client, and

- In the case of MiFID or equivalent third country business, provides 'express confirmation' of their agreement (which may be for a specific transaction or may be general) to be treated as an eligible counterparty

If the prospective counterparty is established in another EEA state, for MiFID business the firm should defer to the status determined by the law of that other state.

2.3 Agent as client

One area that has proved complicated in the past is where a firm is dealing with an **agent**. For example, suppose that a solicitor is acting for his client and approaches a firm to sell bonds on his client's behalf. Clearly, it is important that the firm establish whether it owes duties to the solicitor or to the solicitor's client.

The agent is the client of the firm, unless an agreement in writing treats the other person as the client.

The relevant COBS rule applies to designated investment business and ancillary services. The rule states that the firm may treat the agent as its client if the agent is another authorised firm or an overseas financial services institution **or** if the agent is another person, provided that the arrangement is not to avoid duties which the firm would otherwise owe to the agent's clients.

An agreement may however be made, in writing, to treat the other person (in the above example, the solicitor's client) as the firm's client.

2.4 Providing a higher level of protection to clients

Firms must allow **professional clients** and **eligible counterparties** to re-categorise in order to get more protection. Such clients are themselves responsible for asking for higher protection if they deem themselves to be **unable** to assess properly or manage the risks involved.

Either on its own initiative or following a client request or written agreement:

- A *per se* **eligible counterparty** may be re-categorised as a **professional client** or **retail client**
- A *per se* **professional client** may be re-categorised as a **retail client**

The **higher level of protection** may be provided through re-categorisation:

- On a general basis
- Trade by trade
- In respect of specified rules
- In respect of particular services, transactions, transaction types or product types

The client should (of course) be notified of a re-categorisation.

Firms must have written internal policies and procedures to categorise clients.

3 CLIENT AGREEMENTS AND INFORMATION PROVISION

3.1 Client agreements: designated investment business

If a firm carries on **designated investment business**, other than advising on investments, for a **new retail client,** the firm must enter into a **basic agreement** with the client. Although little guidance is given in the rules as to the contents, the agreement will set out the essential rights and obligations of the firm, and must be in writing – on paper or other durable medium. For a **professional client**, there is no requirement for an agreement, although most firms will wish there to be one.

In good time, normally **before** the client is bound by any agreement relating to designated investment business or ancillary services, the firm must provide to the retail client – either in a durable medium or on a website, if the website conditions are satisfied:

- The terms of the agreement
- Information about **the firm and its services** (see below), including information on communications, conflicts of interest and authorised status

The agreement and information may be provided **immediately after** the client is bound by the agreement if the agreement was concluded using a means of distance communication (e.g. telephone).

Relevant material changes to the information provided must be notified to the client in **good time**.

3.2 Information disclosure before providing services

earning objective **Know** the requirement to provide information to clients prior to providing services to clients including information relating to the nature and risk of the services and designated investments being offered

A firm must provide to clients appropriate in...

- The **firm and its services**
- Designated investments a... **risks** associated with de...
- Execution venues
- Costs and associated charges

The information on designated investments and proposed investment strategies must be provided for MiFID business, and also for non-MiFID designated investment business in relation to **derivatives, warrants** and **stock lending activity**.

3.3 Information about a firm and its services

Information about a firm and its services which must be provided to a **retail client** comprises the following general information:

- The firm's **name and address**, and **contact details** which allow effective communication
- For MiFID and equivalent third country business, the **languages** the firm uses for documents and other communication
- **Methods of communication with clients** which are used by the firm, including those for sending and receiving orders where relevant
- Statement that the firm is **authorised**, and the name of the authorising **competent authority** (e. g. the Financial Services Authority) – with the authority's contact address, in the case of MiFID business
- If the firm is acting through an **appointed representative or tied agent**, a statement of this fact specifying the EEA state in which the representative/agent is registered
- The nature, frequency and timing of **performance reports** provided by the firm (in accordance with rules on reporting to clients)
- For a common platform firm or a third country (non-EEA) investment firm, the firm's **conflicts of interest policy** (or a summary of it)
- For non-common platform firms, details of **how the firm will ensure fair treatment** of clients when material interests or conflicts of interest arise

3.4 Information about designated investments

The provisions in this section apply to **MiFID** and equivalent third country business, and also to the **following regulated activities** when they involve a **retail client**.

- Making a personal recommendation about a designated investment
- Managing designated investments
- Arranging or executing a deal in warrants or derivatives
- Stock lending activity

Firms must provide to clients a **general description of the nature and risks** of the type of designated investments involved, taking into account the client's categorisation as a **retail** or **professional** client.

Each of a series on transactions involving the same type of investment does not need to be treated as a new or different service. However, if product charges differ from those already disclosed, the new details must be given. A **key features document** or **simplified prospectus** may meet the requirements of this section. Information must be provided in a durable medium, or via a website meeting the website conditions.

The description must be in enough detail to enable the client to make investment decisions on an informed basis, including where relevant for the investment type and status and knowledge of the client:

- **Risks** associated with that type of designated investment, explaining **leverage** and its effects, and the risk of losing the entire investment

- **Price volatility** of designated investments and any **limitations on the available market**

- Financial commitments such as **contingent liabilities** which may be assumed as a result of transactions

- Any applicable **margin requirements** (e. g. money which must be deposited to cover potential losses as the price of derivatives changes)

For a designated investment subject to a current offer to the public, where a **prospectus** has been published, the firm must inform the client that the prospectus has been published.

Where a designated investment is **composed of two or more designated investments** and is likely to carry greater **risks** than the components, the firm must describe how the **interaction** of the components increases risk.

For a designated investment incorporating a **guarantee by a third party**, sufficient information must be given about the guarantor and the guarantee to enable the retail client to assess it.

3.5 Provision of information: managing investments

Learning objective	**Know** the rules on the provision of information in connection with the services of managing investments

A firm **managing investments** must establish a **benchmark** or other appropriate method of evaluation and comparison, based on the client's investment objectives and the designated investments in their portfolio, to enable the client to assess the firm's performance.

Firms proposing to **manage investments** for a **retail client** must provide the following information to the client:

- Method and frequency of valuation of designated investments in the client's portfolio
- Details of any delegation of the discretionary management of the investments
- Specification of any benchmark used to compare performance
- Types of designated investments and transactions that may be included in the portfolio
- Management objectives, the level of risk reflected, and any constraints in the manager's discretion

3.6 Information on safeguards and client money

earning objective **Know** the rules on the provision of information concerning safeguarding of designated investments belonging to clients and client money

A firm holding **designated investments** or **client money** for a **retail client** subject to MiFID custody and client money rules must provide the following information to clients where applicable:

- That the investments/money may be held by a third party on behalf of the firm

- The responsibility of the firm for acts or omissions of the third party, under national laws

- Consequences for the client of the insolvency of the third party

- If the designated investments belonging to the retail client are held in an omnibus account by a third party (in which case, there should be a prominent warning of the resulting risks)

- If the designated investments cannot, under national law, be separately identified from the firm or the third party, a prominent warning of the resulting risks

- Client rights relating to accounts subject to jurisdiction outside the EEA

- Summary of steps taken to protect the client's investments/money, including summary details of any investor compensation scheme which applies (professional clients must also be given this information)

- Any security interest, lien or right of set-off held by a depositary (again, for professional clients as well as retail, in this case)

Before **using clients' designated investments for its own account**, a firm must provide in good time and in a durable medium clear full and accurate information on the firm's obligations and responsibilities with respect to that use, including terms for restitution and risks involved.

3.7 Information about costs, charges and compensation

earning objective **Know** the rules on disclosure of costs and associated charges, timing of disclosure, medium of disclosure, changes to information provided to the client and compensation information

3.7.1 Information about costs and charges

Firms must provide information on **costs and associated charges** to retail clients, including:

- The total price to be paid by the client (or the basis for calculation, if an exact price cannot be indicated) for the designated investments or ancillary services including all related fees, commissions (separately itemised), charges, expenses and taxes payable via the firm (with currency exchange rates where relevant)

- Notice of the possibility that other costs not paid via the firm, including taxes, may arise

- Payment arrangements

3.7.2 Compensation information

For MiFID business, the firm must tell the client about the applicable **investor compensation scheme**, giving information in a durable medium or via a website meeting the website conditions and in the language of the EEA state:

- On the amount and scope of cover offered
- At the client's request, on conditions and formalities involved in claiming compensation

3.8 Medium of disclosure and changes to information

Information we have described so far in Section 3 of this chapter is to be provided **in good time before providing** designated investment business or ancillary services, or **immediately after starting** to provide the **services** if the agreement was concluded using a means of distance communication.

The information should be provided in a **durable medium**, or via a **website** where the website conditions are satisfied.

The firm must keep the client **notified** in good time of material relevant changes, using a durable medium if that was used initially.

3.9 Information disclosure for packaged products

Learning objective	**Know** the rules on disclosure of information regarding packaged products

3.9.1 Packaged products

'**Packaged products**' relates to products that can be bought 'off-the-shelf', with the terms and conditions and price identical for all potential investors. These are typically products sold through an intermediary, for example an Independent Financial Adviser (IFA).

A **packaged product** is defined as one of the following:

- A life policy
- A unit in a regulated collective investment scheme
- An interest in an investment trust savings scheme
- A stakeholder pension scheme
- A personal pension scheme

whether or not (in the case of the first three types listed above) it is held within a PEP, an ISA or a Child Trust Fund (CTF) and whether or not the packaged product is also a stakeholder product.

Exam tip	Use the word **CLIPS** to remember the types of packaged product.
	    Collective Investment Schemes (regulated)
	    Life policies
	    Investment trust savings schemes
	    Personal pensions
	    Stakeholder pensions

There are disclosure rules, described below, which apply when a firm makes a **personal recommendation** to a **retail client** to buy a **packaged product**. These rules do not apply when special rules on (scripted) **basic advice** for stakeholder products are being followed.

These rules apply to a UK firm's business carried out in another EEA State for a retail client in the UK, subject to certain exclusions. They also apply to business carried out in the UK for a client in another EEA state.

3.9.2 Selling products from the scope

The firm's disclosures should indicate whether it expects its **scope** to be:

- The whole of the market or market sector
- Limited to several product providers
- Limited to a single product provider

In accordance with the **client's best interests rule** and the **fair, clear and not misleading rule**, a firm must ensure that:

- Its representatives consider, based on adequate knowledge, products across its scope

- Products outside the scope are not recommended

- All representatives advising on packaged products and making recommendations can recommend and sell each product in the relevant range. (If a representative is not competent to advise on a product or category, a client to whom a recommendation ought to be made should be referred to a representative who is competent.)

- The scope disclosed to the client is not narrowed without appropriate new disclosure to the client

- The scope is not extended in a way that alters remuneration arrangements unless it provides new disclosures on inducements, charges and costs (e. g. by providing a further '**menu**')

3.9.3 Disclosures to retail clients: IDD and 'Menu'

For packaged products business, the retail client must be provided with an **initial disclosure document (IDD)** and **menu**, or a combined IDD, in a durable medium. (The combined IDD is for cases where home finance as well as other business is being provided.) The firm should consider whether an IDD or menu need to be provided if they were provided previously and still apply.

The IDD and combined IDD are documents containing:

- The keyfacts logo
- Specified headings and text (see the example below)

Standard wordings are provided for those drafting IDDs and menus, at the Forms link ('Conduct of Business Forms') in the FSA website at **www.fsahandbook.info**.

The FSA considers that the disclosure requirements are met if the firm's representatives provide these documents '**in good time**' before the client is bound by an agreement to provide a personal recommendation, or the firm performs an act preparatory to providing a recommendation.

3.9.4 Initial disclosure document

An example of an **IDD** is shown below.

Keyfacts about our services

XYZ **Independent Financial Services Ltd**	2 More Road, Any Town, W1 0TB

1. The Financial Services Authority (FSA)

The FSA is the independent watchdog that regulates financial services. It requires us to give you this document. Use this information to decide if our services are right for you.

2. Whose products do we offer?

✓	We offer products from the whole market.
	We only offer products from a limited number of companies.
	We only offer products from a single group of companies.

3. Which services will we provide you with?

✓	We will advise and make a recommendation for you after we have assessed your needs.
	You will not receive advice or a recommendation from us. We may ask some questions to narrow down the selection of products that we will provide details on. You will need to make your own choice about how to proceed.
	We will provide basic advice on a limited range of stakeholder products and in order to do this we will ask some questions about your income, savings and other circumstances, but we will not ■ Conduct a full assessment of your needs. ■ Offer advice on whether a non-stakeholder product may be more suitable.

4. What will you have to pay us for our services?

✓	Before we provide you with advice, we will give you our **keyfacts** guide '**about the cost of our services**'.
	We will tell you how we get paid, and the amount, before we carry out any business for you.

---

5. **Who regulates us?**

- **XYZ Independent Financial Services Ltd**, 2 More Road, Any Town, W1 0TB is authorized and regulated by the Financial Services Authority. Our FSA Register number is 123007.

- Our permitted business is **advising and arranging life insurance, pensions and unit trust business**.

- You can check this on the FSA's Register by visiting the FSA's website www.fsa.gov.uk/register or by contacting the FSA on 0845 606 1234.

6. **Loans and ownership**

- Bizee Life Office Ltd owns 25% of our share capital.

- We have 20% of the voting rights in Royal Edinburgh.

7. **What to do if you have a complaint**

- If you wish to register a complaint, please contact us:

  In writing: Complaints Department, XYZ Independent Financial Services Ltd, 2 More Road, Any Town, W1 0TB

  By phone: 0121 100 1234

- If you cannot settle your complaint with us, you may be entitled to refer it to the Financial Ombudsman Service.

8. **Are we covered by the Financial Services Compensation Scheme (FSCS)?**

- We are covered by the FSCS. You may be entitled to compensation from the scheme if we cannot meet our obligations. This depends on the type of business and the circumstances of the claim.

- Most type of investment business are covered for 100% of the first £30,000 and 90% of the next £20,000 – so the maximum compensation is £48,000.

- Further information about compensation scheme arrangements is available from the FSCS.

The firm may include, at the end of the IDD, disclosure of a tied agent's capacity.

3.9.5 The 'Menu'

The **menu** is entitled **'Key Facts: A Guide to the Cost of our Services'** and includes:

- A section on the FSA, and the purpose of the required menu
- A section in which the firm gives details of 'Our services'
- The payment options offered (whether paying by fee or by commission/product charges)
- The typical fees or maximum commission the firm is likely to receive for a transaction
- An indication of the market average commission (for commission-based work)

The **market average (MA)** is designed to give consumers a benchmark for what might be a competitive level of commission.

An adviser should not start charging until after the customer has been given a menu and has agreed the **payment option** for the client.

It is acceptable for a firm to have different 'menus', and firms are free to offer different charging structures to different groups of clients.

If a firm did not provide information on expected commission arrangements in the menu, it would be unlikely to be in compliance with the **client's best interests rule**.

3.9.6 Providing requested information

A firm's representative should provide a **copy** of the appropriate range of packaged products to the client, on the client's **request**.

3.9.7 Ongoing disclosure

Firms should not arrange to retain commission in excess of the maximum rate previously disclosed without providing **further inducements information** to the client, and obtaining the client's informed consent to the alteration, in a durable medium.

3.10 Reliance on others

Learning objective	**Know** the rules, guidance and evidential provisions regarding reliance on others

Suppose that a firm (**F1**) carrying out MiFID or equivalent third country business receives an instruction from an investment firm (**F2**) to perform an investment or ancillary service on behalf of a client (**C**).

F1 may rely on:

- Information about the client **C** which firm **F2** provides
- Recommendations about the service provided to **C** by **F2**

F2 remains responsible for the completeness and accuracy of information provided and the appropriateness of its advice.

More generally, a firm is taken to be in **compliance with COBS** rules which require it to obtain information, if it can show it was **reasonable** for it to rely on information provided by others in writing. It is reasonable to rely on written information provided by another where that person is **competent** and **not connected** with the firm.

This rule links with Principle 2 *Skill, Care and Diligence*. Note that this rule has no impact on the requirements laid down in the Money Laundering Regulations, which require a firm to identify its clients for money laundering purposes.

4   COMMUNICATING WITH CLIENTS

Learning objectives	**Know** the application of the rules on communication to clients, including financial promotions and firms' responsibilities for appointed representatives
	Know the purpose and application of the financial promotion rules and the relationship with Principles for Businesses 6 and 7
	Know the types and methods of communication addressed by COBS 4

4.1 Introduction

A **financial promotion** is an **invitation** or **inducement** to engage in investment activity. The term therefore describes most forms and methods of marketing financial services. It covers traditional advertising, most website content, telephone sales campaigns and face-to-face meetings. The term is extended to cover **marketing communications** by MiFID.

BPP
LEARNING MEDIA

The purpose of regulation in this area is to create a regime where the quality of financial promotions is scrutinised by an authorised firm who must then comply with lengthy rules to ensure that their promotions are **clear**, **fair and not misleading** (Principle 7) and that customers are treated **fairly** (Principle 6).

4.2 Application of the financial promotions rules

The **financial promotions rules** within COBS apply to a firm:

- Communicating with a **client** in relation to **designated investment business**

- **Communicating** or **approving** a **financial promotion** (with some exceptions in respect of: credit promotions, home purchase plans, home reversion schemes, non-investment insurance contracts and unregulated collective investment schemes)

Firms must also apply the rules to promotions issued by their **appointed representatives**.

4.3 Territorial scope

For financial promotions, the **general application rule** applies. This indicates that the rules apply to a firm in respect of designated investment business carried out from an establishment maintained by the firm or its appointed representative in the UK. Additionally, in general the rules apply to firms carrying on business with a client in the UK from an establishment overseas.

The financial promotions rules also apply to:

- Promotions communicated to a person in the UK

- Cold (unsolicited) calling to someone outside the UK, if the call is from within the UK or is in respect of UK business

4.4 Fair, clear and not misleading

Learning objective	**Know** the rule on fair, clear and not misleading communications and the guidance on fair, clear and not misleading financial promotions

A firm must ensure that a communication or financial promotion is **fair, clear and not misleading**, as is **appropriate** and **proportionate** considering the means of communication and the information to be conveyed.

This rule applies to **communications** in relation to designated investment business other than a third party prospectus.

It applies to **financial promotions** approved by the firm, and to financial promotions communicated by the firm which are not non-retail, or excluded and are not a third party prospectus.

Note that additionally **s397 FSMA 2000** creates a criminal offence relating to **certain misleading statements and practices**, as explained in Chapter 2 of this Study Book.

The **fair, clear and not misleading rule** is specifically interpreted in COBS as it applies to financial promotions in some aspects, as follows.

- If a product or service places a client's capital at risk, this should be made clear

- Any yield figure quoted should give a balanced impression of both short-term and long-term prospects for the investment

- Sufficient information must be provided to explain any complex charging arrangements, taking into account recipients' needs

- The regulator (FSA) should be named, and any non-regulated aspects made clear

- A fair, clear and not misleading impression should be given of the producer for any packaged or stakeholder products not produced by the firm

The British Bankers' Association / Building Societies Association **Code of Conduct for the Advertising of Interest Bearing Accounts** is also relevant in the case of financial promotions relating to deposits.

4.5 Identifying promotions as such

Learning objective	Know the rule on identifying promotions as such

A firm must ensure that a **financial promotion** addressed to a **client** is clearly **identifiable as such**.

- This rule does not apply to a third party prospectus in respect of **MiFID** (or equivalent third country) business.

- There are also some exceptions in respect of **non-MiFID** business, including prospectus advertisements, image advertising, non-retail communications, deposits and pure protection long-term care insurance (LTCI) products.

4.6 Exceptions

Learning objective	Know the main exceptions to the financial promotions rules in COBS (and the glossary definition of 'excluded communications'), the limitations in connection to MiFID business and the existence of the Financial Promotions Order

As mentioned earlier, the **financial promotions rules** in COBS do **not apply** to promotions of qualifying credit, home purchase plans, home reversion schemes, non-investment insurance contracts, and certain unregulated collective investment schemes whose promotions firms may not communicate or approve.

Except in regard to disclosure of compensation arrangements, the COBS rules on communications (including financial promotions) do **not** apply when a firm communicates with an **eligible counterparty**.

The financial promotions rules also do **not** apply to incoming communications in relation to **MiFID business** of an investment firm **from another EEA state** that are, in its home state, regulated under MiFID.

4.7 Excluded communications

A firm may rely on one or more of the following aspects which make a communication into an **excluded communication** for the purposes of the rules.

- A financial promotion that would benefit from an exemption in the Financial Promotion Order (see below) if it were communicated by an unauthorised person, or which originates outside the UK and has no effect in the UK

- A financial promotion from outside the UK that would be exempt under articles 30, 31, 32 or 33 of the Financial Promotion Order (Overseas communicators) if the office from which the financial promotion is communicated were a separate unauthorised person

- A financial promotion that is subject to, or exempted from, the Takeover Code or to the requirements relating to takeovers or related operations in another EEA state

- A personal quotation or illustration form

- A **'one-off' financial promotion** that is not a cold call. The following conditions indicate that the promotion is a 'one-off', but they need not necessarily be present for a promotion to be considered as 'one-off'.

    (i)   The financial promotion is communicated only to one recipient or only to one group of recipients in the expectation that they would engage in any investment activity jointly

    (ii)   The identity of the product or service to which the financial promotion relates has been determined having regard to the particular circumstances of the recipient

    (iii)   The financial promotion is not part of an organised marketing campaign

4.8 Financial Promotions Order

Section 21 FSMA 2000 makes it criminal for someone to undertake a financial promotion, i.e. invite or induce another to engage in investment activity, unless they are either:

- An **authorised firm** (i.e. **issuing the financial promotion**), or
- The content of the communication is **approved** by an authorised firm

Contravention of section 21 is punishable by up to **two** years in jail and an **unlimited** fine.

There are a number of exemptions from s21 set out in the **Financial Promotions Order**. The effect of being an **exemption** is that the promotion would **not** need to be issued or approved by an authorised firm. It would therefore not have to comply with the detailed financial promotion rules.

The main examples are as follows. (Other exemptions cover certain one-off and purely factual promotions.)

Exemption	Comments
1. Investment professional	A communication to an authorised or exempt person.
2. Deposits and insurance	Very limited application of COBS.
3. Certified high net worth individuals	Anyone may promote **unlisted securities** to persons who hold certificates of high net worth (normally signed by their accountant or employer, however, these can now be self-certified by an individual) and who have agreed to be classified as such. Requirements for a certificate are that a person must have a net income of £100,000 or more, or net assets (excluding principal property) of £250,000 or more. Note that, if applicable, the financial promotion should not invite or induce the recipient to engage in business with the firm that signed the certificate of high net worth.
4. Associations of high net worth individuals	Anyone can promote non-derivative products to associations of high net worth investors.
5. Sophisticated investors	Anyone can promote products to a person who holds a certificate indicating that they are knowledgeable in a particular stock (normally signed by an authorised firm, however, individuals can now self-certify themselves as sophisticated in relation to unlisted securities) and who have signed a statement agreeing to be such. Note that the financial promotion should not invite or induce the recipient to engage in business with the authorised firm that signed the certificate.
6. Takeover Code	Promotions subject to the Takeover Code.

4.9 Prospectus advertisements

Learning objective **Know** the rules on prospectus advertisements

Where a **prospectus** is issued on an offer or an admission of transferable securities to trading, there are rules governing advertisements relating to it.

The **advertisement**:

- Must state that a prospectus has been or will be published, and indicate where it can be obtained
- Must be clearly recognisable as an advertisement
- Must not contain inaccurate or misleading information
- Must be consistent with information in the prospectus

A written advertisement should contain a **bold and prominent statement** indicating that it is not a prospectus but an advertisement and that investors should not subscribe for transferable securities mentioned except on the basis of information in the prospectus.

All information issued – oral or written, even if not for advertising purposes – must be consistent with the prospectus.

4.10 Communicating with retail clients

Learning objective **Know** the general rule in connection with communicating with retail clients

4.10.1 General rule

The general rule on **communicating with retail clients** in relation to **designated investment business** states that firms must ensure that the information:

- Includes the **name of the firm** (which may be the **trading name** or **shortened name**, provided the firm is identifiable)

- Is accurate and does not emphasise potential benefits of investment without also giving a **fair and prominent indication of relevant risks**

- Is **sufficient** for and presented so as to be **likely to be understood** by the **average member** of the group to whom it is directed or by whom it is likely to be received

- Does **not disguise, diminish** or **obscure** important **items, statements** or **warnings**

In deciding whether and how to communicate to a target audience, the firm should **consider**: the nature of the product/business, risks, the client's commitment, the average recipient's information needs and the role of the information in the sales process.

The firm should consider whether omission of a relevant fact will result in information being **insufficient, unclear, unfair** or **misleading**.

4.10.2 Comparative information

Information comparing business / investments / persons must:

- Present **comparisons** in a meaningful, fair and balanced way

- In relation to MiFID or equivalent third country business, specify **information sources**, key facts and assumptions

4.10.3 Tax treatment

If **tax treatment** is referred to, it should be stated prominently that the tax treatment depends on the individual circumstances of the client and may be subject to change in future. (One of a couple of exceptions to this rule is that it does not apply to deposits other than cash ISAs or CTFs.)

4.10.4 Consistency

The firm should ensure that information in a financial promotion is **consistent** with other information provided to the retail client. (**Deposits** are an exception to this rule.)

4.11 Past, simulated past and future information

Learning objective **Know** the rules on past, simulated past and future performance information

4.11.1 Introduction

Rules on **performance information** apply to information disseminated to retail clients, and to financial promotions. In the case of non-MiFID business, the rules do not apply to deposits generally nor to pure protection long-term care insurance (LTCI) contracts.

4.11.2 Past performance information

Past performance information must:

- **Not** be the most prominent feature of the communication

- Include appropriate information covering at least the **five preceding years**, or the whole period the investment/service has been offered/provided or the whole period the financial index has been established, if less than five years

- Be based on and must show complete **12-month periods**

- State the **reference period** and **source of the information**

- Contain a **prominent warning** that the figures refer to the past and that past performance is not a reliable indicator of future results

- If denominated in a foreign **currency**, state the currency clearly, with a warning that the return may increase or decrease as a result of currency fluctuations

- If based on gross performance, disclose the effect of **commissions**, fees or other charges

The above provisions are to be interpreted in a way that is '**appropriate and proportionate**' to the communication. For example, in a periodic statement issued for investments managed, past performance may be the most prominent feature, in spite of the first bullet point immediately above.

For a **packaged product** (except a unitised with-profits life policy or a stakeholder pension scheme), information should be given on:

- An **offer to bid** basis (which should be stated) for an actual return or comparison with other investments, or

- An **offer to offer**, **bid to bid** or **offer to bid** basis (which should be stated) if there is a comparison with an index or with movements in the price of units, or

- A **single pricing** basis with allowance for charges

4.11.3 Simulated past performance information

Simulated past performance information must:

- Relate to an investment or a financial index

- Be based on actual past performance of investments/indices which are the same as, or underlie, the investment concerned

- Contain a **prominent warning** that figures refer to simulated past performance and that past performance is not a reliable indicator of future performance

4.11.4 Future performance information

Future performance information must:

- **Not** be based on nor refer to simulated past performance
- Be based on **reasonable assumptions** supported by **objective data**
- If based on gross performance, disclose the effect of **commissions**, fees or other charges
- Contain a **prominent warning** that such forecasts are not a reliable indicator of future performance
- Only be provided if **objective data** can be obtained

4.12 Financial promotions containing offers or invitations

Learning objective	**Know** the rule on financial promotions containing offers or invitations

A **direct offer financial promotion** is a form of financial promotion which enables investors to purchase investments directly 'off the page' without receiving further information.

A direct offer financial promotion to retail clients must contain whatever **disclosures** are relevant to that offer or invitation (as outlined earlier, such as information about the firm and its services, and costs and charges) and, for non-MiFID business, additional appropriate information about the relevant business and investments so that the client is reasonably able to understand their nature and risks, and consequently to take investment decisions on an informed basis. This information may be contained in a separate document to which the client must refer in responding to the offer or invitation. Alternatively, information disclosures may be omitted if the firm can demonstrate that the client referred to the required information before making or accepting the offer.

A firm may wish to include in a direct offer financial promotion a summary of **tax** consequences, and a statement that the recipient should seek a **personal recommendation** if he has any doubt about the suitability of the investments or services.

4.13 Unwritten promotions and cold calling

Learning objective	**Know** the rules on unwritten promotions and the restriction on cold calling

An **unwritten financial promotion** outside the firm's premises may only be initiated if the person communicating it:

- Does so at an appropriate time of day

- Identifies himself and his firm, and makes his purpose clear

- Clarifies if the client wants to continue or terminate the communication, and terminates it on request at any time

- If an appointment is arranged, gives a contact point to a client

Firms may only make **cold (unsolicited) calls** if:

- The recipient has an established client relationship with the firm, such that the recipient envisages receiving them, or

- The call is about a generally marketed packaged product (not based on a high volatility fund), or

- The call relates to controlled activities by an authorised person or exempt person, involving only readily realisable securities (not warrants)

4.14 Financial promotions for the business of overseas persons

Know the rule on financial promotions for overseas persons

An 'overseas person' here means a firm carrying on regulated activities who does not do so within the UK.

Any financial promotion for the business of such an **overseas person** must:

- Make clear which firm has approved or communicated it

- Explain that rules for protection of retail clients do not apply

- Explain the extent and level of any available compensation scheme (or state that no scheme applies)

- Not be issued if the firm has any reason to doubt that the overseas person will deal with UK retail clients in an honest and reliable way

4.15 Approving financial promotions

Know the requirement for approving financial promotions and the circumstances of relying on another firm's confirmation of compliance

The rules in **SYSC** require that a firm which communicates with a client regarding designated investment business, or communicates or approves a financial promotion, puts in place **systems and controls** or **policies and procedures** in order to comply with the COBS rules.

Section 21(1) FSMA 2000 prohibits an unauthorised person from communicating a financial promotion, unless either an exemption applies or the financial promotion is approved by an authorised firm.

Approval of a financial promotion by an **authorised firm** enables it to be communicated by an **unauthorised firm**.

A firm **approving** a financial promotion must confirm that it **complies** with the **financial promotion rules**. The firm must withdraw its approval, and notify anyone it knows to be relying on its approval, if it becomes aware that it no longer complies with the financial promotion rules.

A promotion made during a personal visit, telephone conversation or other interactive dialogue cannot be approved.

Approval given by the firm may be '**limited**', e.g. limited to communication to **professional clients** or **eligible counterparties**.

In communicating a financial promotion, a firm is permitted to **rely on another firm's confirmation of compliance** with the financial promotions rules. The firm must take reasonable care to ensure that the promotion is only communicated to types of recipients for whom it was intended.

5 ADVISING AND SELLING

5.1 Assessing suitability

Suitability rules apply when a firm makes a **personal recommendation** in relation to a **designated investment** (but not if the firm makes use of the rules on basic scripted advice for stakeholder products).

The firm has obligations regarding the assessment of **suitability**: the firm must take reasonable steps to ensure that, in respect of designated investments, a personal recommendation or a decision to trade is **suitable for its client**.

To meet this obligation, the firm must **obtain necessary information** regarding the client's:

- **Knowledge and experience** in the relevant investment field (including: types of investment or service with which the client is familiar; transactions experience; level of education and profession or former profession; understanding of risks)

- **Investment objectives** (including: length of time he wishes to hold the investment; risk preferences; risk profile; purposes of the investment)

- **Financial situation** (including: extent and source of regular income; assets including liquid assets; investments and real property; regular financial commitments) (Is he able to bear any investment risks, consistent with his investment objectives?)

The firm is entitled to **rely on information provided by the client**, unless it is aware that the information is out of date, inaccurate or incomplete.

A **transaction** may be **unsuitable** for a client because of:

- The risks of the designated investments involved
- The type of transaction
- The characteristics of the order
- The frequency of trading
- It resulting in an unsuitable portfolio (in the case of **managing investments**)

For non-MiFID business, these rules apply to business with **retail clients**. When making personal recommendations or managing investments for **professional clients**, in the course of MiFID or equivalent third country business, a firm is entitled to assume that the client has the necessary experience and knowledge, in relation to products and services for which the professional client is so classified.

BPP
LEARNING MEDIA

5.2 Suitability report

Understand the obligation to provide a retail client with a suitability report

Know the timing and contents of a suitability report

5.2.1 Requirement

A firm must provide a **suitability report** to a retail client if the firm makes a personal recommendation and the client:

- Buys or sells shares/units in a regulated collective investment scheme

- Buys or sells shares through an investment trust savings scheme or investment trust ISA or PEP

- Buys, sells, surrenders, cancels rights in or suspends contributions to a personal or stakeholder pension scheme

- Elects to make income withdrawals from a short-term annuity

- Enters into a pension transfer or pension opt-out

A suitability report is required for all personal recommendations in relation to **life policies**.

A suitability report is **not** required:

- If the firm acts as investment manager and recommends a regulated collective investment scheme

- If the client is habitually resident outside the EEA and is not in the UK when acknowledging consent to the proposal form

- For small life policies (not >£50 p.a.) recommended by friendly societies

- For recommendations to increase regular premiums on an existing contract

- For recommendations to invest further single contributions to an existing packaged product

5.2.2 Timing

The suitability report must generally be provided to the client **as soon as possible after the transaction is effected**. For personal or stakeholder pension schemes requiring notification of cancellation rights, the report must be provided no later than 14 days after the contract is concluded.

5.2.3 Contents

The suitability report must, at least:

- Specify the client's **demands and needs**

- Explain the firm's **recommendation** that the transaction is suitable, having regard to information provided by the client

- Explain any possible **disadvantages** of the transaction to the client

The firm should give details appropriate to the **complexity** of the transaction.

For **income withdrawals** from a **short-term annuity**, the explanation of possible disadvantages should include **risk factors** involved in income withdrawals or purchase of a short-term annuity.

5.3 Advising on packaged products

Learning objective	**Know** the application and purpose of the rules on advising on packaged products, including the scope and range of advising

We looked at aspects of **packaged products** earlier in this Chapter when we considered information disclosure. Additional points are outlined below.

As we saw earlier, the firm's disclosures should indicate whether it expects its scope to be:

- The whole of the market or market sector
- Limited to several product providers
- Limited to a single product provider

What is meant by the **scope** and **range** of a firm's advice?

- The **scope** relates to the **product providers** whose products it sells
- The **range** relates to which **products** from those providers it sells

A firm must maintain an up-to-date **record** of the **scopes and ranges** it uses, and must keep the records for at least **five years**.

If a firm holds itself out as independent or with a scope across the whole market or a whole market sector, the firm's selection will need to be '**sufficiently large**' to satisfy the client's best interests rule and the fair, clear and not misleading rule. (Note how, similarly to many other cases, the rules do not specify the meaning of 'sufficiently large'. In line with principles-based regulation, it is up to the firm to come to a judgement on how it can comply.)

A firm may use sufficient '**panels' of product providers** to cover the whole of the market, and if so should review these regularly.

A firm holding itself out as providing personal recommendations from the whole market on personal pension schemes must cover all types of such scheme, including **self-invested personal pension schemes (SIPPs)**.

5.4 Appropriateness

Learning objectives	**Understand** the application and purpose of the rules on non-advised sales
	Understand the obligations for assessing appropriateness
	Know the obligation to warn the client
	Know the circumstances in which it is not necessary to assess appropriateness

The **appropriateness** rules we outline here apply to a firm providing **investment services** in the course of **MiFID** or equivalent third country business, **other than** making a personal recommendation and managing investments. The rules thus apply to '**execution only**' services which are available in the UK, where transactions are undertaken at the initiative of the customer without advice having been given. (Note that, as we have seen, the **suitability** rules apply where there is a personal recommendation.) One firm may rely on another MiFID firm's assessment of appropriateness, in line with the general rule on reliance on other investment firms.

The rules apply to arranging or dealing in **derivatives** or **warrants** for a **retail client**, when in response to a **direct offer financial promotion**.

To **assess appropriateness**, the firm must ask the client to provide information on his knowledge and experience in the relevant investment field, to enable the assessment to be made.

The firm will then:

- Determine whether the client has the necessary **experience and knowledge** to understand the **risks** involved in the product/service (including the following aspects: nature and extent of service with which client is familiar; complexity; risks involved; extent of client's transactions in designated investments; level of client's education and profession or former profession)

- Be entitled to assume that a **professional client** has such experience and knowledge, for products/services for which it is classified as 'professional'

Unless it knows the information from the client to be out-of-date, inaccurate or incomplete, the firm may rely on it. Where reasonable, a firm may infer knowledge from experience.

The firm may seek to increase the client's level of understanding by providing appropriate information to the client.

If the firm is satisfied about the client's experience and knowledge, there is **no duty to communicate** this to the client. If, in doing so, it is making a personal recommendation, it must comply with the **suitability** rules. But if the firm concludes that the product or service is **not appropriate** to the client, it must **warn** the client. The warning may be in a standardised format.

If the client provides insufficient information, the firm must **warn** the client that such a decision will not allow the firm to determine whether the service or product is appropriate for him. Again, the warning may be in a standardised format.

If a client who has received a warning asks the firm to go ahead with the transaction, it is for the firm to consider whether to do so 'having regard to the circumstances'.

5.5 When is an assessment of appropriateness not needed?

A firm does **not** need to seek information from the client or assess appropriateness if:

- The service consists only of execution and receiving / transmitting client orders for particular **financial instruments** (see below), provided at the initiative of the client

- The client has been informed clearly that in providing this service the firm is not required to assess suitability and that therefore he does not receive protection from the suitability rules, and

- The firm complies with obligations regarding conflicts of interest

The particular **financial instruments** are:

- Shares on a regulated or equivalent third country market

- Money market instruments, bonds and other forms of securitised debt (excluding bonds and securitised debt which embed a derivative)

- Units in a UCITS scheme

- Other non-complex financial instruments (among the requirements to qualify as 'non-complex' are that they cannot lead the investor to lose more than they invested, adequate information is freely available, there is a market for them with prices made available independently of the issuer, and they do not give rise to cash settlement in the way that many derivatives do)

For a **course of dealings** in a specific type of product or service, the firm does not have to make a new assessment for each transaction.

If a client has engaged in a **course of dealings before 1 November 2007**, he is presumed to have the necessary experience and knowledge to understand the risks involved.

A firm need not assess appropriateness if it is receiving or transmitting and order for which it has assessed **suitability** under the COBS suitability rules (covered above). Also, a firm may not need to assess appropriateness if it is able to rely on a recommendation made by a **different investment firm**.

6 PRODUCT DISCLOSURE AND CANCELLATION RIGHTS

6.1 Key features documents

Know the purpose of the rule on the sale of packaged products to retail clients, the rule requiring the provision of key features to retail clients and the main features to be explained in the key features

6.1.1 Requirement

A firm must prepare a **key features document** for each packaged product, cash deposit ISA and cash deposit CTF it produces, in good time before that document has to be provided.

The firm does **not** have to prepare the document if **another firm** has agreed to prepare it. There are some further **exceptions**, including certain collective investment schemes for which a simplified prospectus is produced instead of a key features document, and stakeholder and personal pension schemes if the information appears prominently in another document.

A **single document** may be used as the key features document for **different schemes**, if the schemes are offered through a '**funds supermarket**' and the document clearly describes the difference between the schemes.

6.1.2 Product information standards

A **key features document** must:

- Be produced / presented to **at least** the quality / standard of **sales and marketing material** used to promote the product

- Display the **firm's brand** as prominently as any other

- Include the **keyfacts logo** prominently at the top

- Include the following **statement**, in a prominent position:

  'The Financial Services Authority is the independent financial services regulator. It requires us, [provider name], to give you this important information to help you to decide whether our [product name] is right for you. You should read this document carefully so that you understand what you are buying, and then keep it safe for future reference.'

- Not include anything that might reasonably cause a retail client to be **mistaken** about the **identity** of the firm that produced, or will produce, the product

6.1.3 Contents of key features document

Required headings in a **key features document** are as follows. (The **order** shown below must be followed.)

- *Title:* '**key features of the [name of product]**'

- *Heading:* '**Its aims**' – followed by a brief description of the product's aims

- *Heading:* '**Your commitment**' or '**Your investment**' – followed by information on what a retail client is committing to or investing in and any consequences of failing to maintain the commitment or investment

- *Heading:* '**Risks**' – followed by information on the material risks associated with the product, including a description of the factors that may have an adverse effect on performance or are material to the decision to invest

- *Heading:* '**Questions and answers**' – (in the form of questions and answers) about the principal terms of the product, what it will do for a retail client and any other information necessary to enable a retail client to make an informed decision

The **key features document** must:

- Include **enough information** about the nature and complexity of the product, any minimum standards / limitations, material benefits / risks of buying or investing for a retail client to be able to make an **informed decision** about whether to proceed

- Explain arrangements for handling **complaints**

- Explain the **compensation** available from the FSCS if the firm cannot meet its liabilities

- Explain whether there are **cancellation / withdrawal rights**, their duration and conditions, including amounts payable if the right is exercised, consequences of not exercising, and practical instructions for exercising the right, including the address to which any notice must be sent

- For **child trust funds (CTFs)**, explain that stakeholder, cash deposit and share CTFs are available, and which type the firm is offering

- For personal pension schemes, explain clearly and prominently that **stakeholder pension schemes** are available and might meet the client's needs as well as the scheme on offer

6.2 Additional information requirements

Note the requirements to provide **general information** to clients about **designated investments**, which were explained earlier in this chapter (at section 3.4 *Information about designated investments*). As we noted there, a **key features document** may meet those requirements.

6.3 Cancellation and withdrawal rights

earning objective **Know** the purpose and requirements of the cancellation and withdrawal rights

6.3.1 Introduction

Cancellation and withdrawal rights are of relevance to firms that enter into a cancellable contract, which means most providers of retail financial products, including distance contracts, based on deposits or designated investments.

6.3.2 Cancellation periods

Minimum **cancellation periods** where a consumer has a right to cancel are summarised below (and are subject to certain exemptions in special situations which are beyond the syllabus). (Note that a **wrapper** means an ISA, PEP or CTF. Personal pension contracts, including SIPPs, and pension contracts based on regulated collective investment schemes, fall within the definition of a **pension wrapper**.)

Life and pensions contracts: 30 calendar days

■ Life policies, including pension annuities, pension policies or within a wrapper (For a life policy effected when opening or transferring a wrapper, the 30-day right applies to the entire arrangement.)

■ Contracts to join a personal or stakeholder pension scheme

■ Pension contracts

■ Pension transfers

■ Initial income withdrawals from an existing personal or stakeholder pension scheme

Cash deposit ISAs: 14 calendar days

Non-life/pensions contracts (advised but not at a distance): 14 calendar days – these rights arise only following a personal recommendation

■ Non-distance contracts to buy units in a regulated collective investment scheme (including within a wrapper or pension wrapper) (For units bought when opening or transferring a wrapper or pension wrapper, the 14-day right applies to the entire arrangement.)

■ Opening or transferring an ISA, PEP or CTF

■ Enterprise Investment Schemes

Non-life/pensions contracts (at a distance): 14 calendar days

■ Accepting deposits
■ Designated investment business

If one transaction attracts more than one right to cancel, the longest period applies.

The **cancellation period begins**:

■ **Either:** From the day the contract is concluded (but, for life policies, when the consumer is informed that the contract has been concluded),

■ **Or:** From the day when the consumer receives the contract terms and conditions, if later

6.3.3 Disclosure of rights to cancel or withdraw

Where the consumer would not already have received similar information under another rule, the firm must **disclose** – in a durable medium and in good time or, if that is not possible, immediately after the consumer is bound – the right to cancel or withdraw, its duration and conditions, information on any further amount payable, consequences of not exercising the right, practical instructions for exercising it, and the address to which notification of cancellation or withdrawal should be sent.

6.3.4 Exercising a right to cancel

A consumer's notification of exercise of a right to cancel is deemed to have observed the deadline if it is **dispatched**, in a durable medium, before the deadline expires.

The consumer need **not** give any **reason** for exercising the right to cancel.

7 DEALING AND MANAGING

7.1 Application of rules

earning objective   **Know** the application of the rules on dealing and managing

COBS includes rules on **dealing and managing**. These rules (except for the rules on personal account dealing – see below) apply to **MiFID business** carried out by a **MiFID investment firm**, and to equivalent third country business.

The provisions on **personal account dealing** apply to designated investment business carried on from a UK establishment. They also apply to passported activities carried on by a UK MiFID investment firm from a branch in another EEA state, but not to the UK branch of an EEA MiFID investment firm in relation to its MiFID business.

7.2 Conflicts of interest

earning objective   **Understand** the application and purpose of the principles and rules on conflict of interest; the rules on identifying conflicts and types of conflicts; the rules on recording and managing conflicts; and the rule on disclosure of conflicts

7.2.1 Principle 8

Inevitably, authorised firms, particularly where they act in dual capacity (both broker and dealing for the firm itself), are faced with **conflicts** between the firm and customers or between one customer and another.

Principle 8 of the *Principles for Businesses* states: 'A firm must manage conflicts of interest fairly, both between itself and its customers and between a customer and another client'.

Principle 8 thus requires that authorised firms should seek to ensure that when **conflicts of interest** do arise, the firm **manages** the conflicts to ensure that customers are treated **fairly**.

7.2.2 SYSC 10

SYSC 10 applies to **common platform firms** carrying on regulated activities and ancillary activities or providing MiFID ancillary services, where a service is provided, to any category of client.

The common platform firm must take all **reasonable steps** to **identify conflicts of interest** between the firm, its managers, employees and appointed representatives or tied agents, or between clients, which may arise in providing a service.

The firm must take into account, as a minimum, likely financial gains, or avoidance of losses, at the expense of a client, interests in the outcome of a service which are different from the client's interest, financial incentives to favour some clients or groups of client, and whether the firm carries on the same business as the client, or receives inducements in the form of monies, goods and services other than the standard commission or fee for that service.

Regularly updated records must be kept of where conflicts of interest have or may arise.

The firm must maintain and operate effective **organisational and administrative arrangements** to prevent conflicts of interest from giving rise to material risk of damage to clients' interests.

Where conflicts are not preventable, the firm must disclose them to clients – in a durable medium, in sufficient detail for the client to take an informed decision – before undertaking business.

Common platform firms should aim to **identify** and **manage** conflicts under a **comprehensive conflicts of interest policy**. That firms actively manage conflicts is important: 'over-reliance of disclosure' without adequate consideration of how to manage conflicts is not permitted.

7.2.3 Conflicts policy

Learning objective **Know** the rule requiring a conflicts policy and the contents of the policy

A **common platform firm** must maintain an effective **conflicts of interest policy**, in **writing** and appropriate to the size and type of firm and its business.

The conflicts of interest policy must:

- Identify circumstances constituting or potentially giving rise to conflicts materially affecting clients
- Specify procedures and measures to manage the conflicts

The procedures and measures must:

- Be designed to ensure that activities are carried on an appropriate **level of independence**

- As and where necessary, include procedures to **prevent and control exchange of information** between persons involved, to **supervise persons separately**, to remove **links in remuneration** producing possible conflicts, to prevent exercise of **inappropriate influence**, and to **prevent and control simultaneous and sequential involvement** of persons in separate services or activities

In drawing up its conflicts policy, the firm must pay **special attention** to the following **activities** (in particular, where persons perform a combination of activities): investment research and advice, proprietary trading, portfolio management and corporate finance business, including underwriting or selling in an offer of securities, and advising on mergers and acquisitions.

In management of an **offering of securities**, the firm might wish to consider agreeing:

- Relevant aspects of the offering process with the corporate finance client at an early stage

- Allocation and pricing objectives with the corporate finance client, inviting the client to participate actively in the allocation process, making the initial recommendation for allocation to retail clients as a single block and not on a named basis and disclosing to the issuer the allocations actually made

7.2.4 'Chinese walls'

Learning objective **Understand** the rules on Chinese walls

Chinese walls are administrative and physical barriers and other internal arrangements, designed to contain **sensitive information**. Most commonly, they are used around the corporate finance departments of firms that often have confidential, sometimes inside, information.

Chinese walls **do not have to be used** by firms, but if they are, this rule becomes relevant.

Where a common platform firm establishes and maintains a Chinese wall, it allows the persons on one side of the wall, e.g. corporate finance, to withhold information from persons on the other side of the wall, e.g. equity research, but only to the extent that one of the parts involves carrying on **regulated activities, ancillary activities** or **MiFID ancillary services**.

A firm will not be guilty of the offences of **Misleading Statements and Practices** (S397 FSMA 2000), **market abuse** I(S 118A(5)(a)) or be liable to a lawsuit under **S150** where the failure arises from the operation of a Chinese wall.

The **effect** of the Chinese walls rule above is that a corporate finance department may have plans for a company that will change the valuation of that company's shares. The equity salesman on the other side of the 'wall' should have no knowledge of these plans; consequently his inability to pass this knowledge on to clients is not seen as a failure of his duty to them.

7.3 Investment research and conflicts of interest

Understand the rules on managing conflicts in connection with investment research and research recommendations

7.3.1 Introduction

There have been concerns that analysts have been encouraged to write favourable research on companies in order to attract lucrative investment banking work. There have also been concerns about firm's employees recommending particular securities while privately trading contrary to the recommendation.

COBS rules on investment research apply to MiFID business carried on by a MiFID investment firm. Rules on disclosure of research recommendations apply to all firms.

7.3.2 Investment research

The rules cover investment research which is intended or likely to be disseminated to clients or to the public.

Firms must ensure that its measures for **managing conflicts of interest** cover the **financial analysts** who produce its investment research, and any other relevant staff.

The firm's arrangements must ensure that:

- The financial analysts and other staff involved do not undertake personal transactions or trade on behalf of other persons, including the firm (unless they are acting as a market maker in good faith), in financial instruments to which unpublished investment research relates, until the **recipients** of the research have had a **reasonable opportunity** to act on it

- In other circumstances, personal transactions by financial analysts and other staff in financial instruments related to investment research they are producing which is **contrary to current recommendations** must only occur in **exceptional circumstances** and with **prior approval** of the firm's legal or compliance function

- The firm and its staff must not **accept inducements** from those with a material interest in the subject matter of investment research, and they must not **promise issuers favourable research coverage**

- Issuers and persons other than financial analysts must not be allowed to **review pre-publication drafts** of investment research for any purpose **other than to verify compliance** with the firm's legal obligations, if the draft includes a recommendation or a target price

There is an exemption from the rules in this section (7.3.2) where a firm distributes investment research **produced by a third party** which is not in the firm's group, provided that the firm does not alter the recommendations and does not present the research as produced by the firm. The firm is required to verify that the independent producer of the research has equivalent arrangements in place to avoid conflicts of interest.

7.3.3 Non-independent research

Investment research is research which Is described as investment research or in similar terms, or is otherwise presented as an objective or independent explanation of the matters contained in the recommendation. Research not meeting this requirement falls within the definition of **non-independent research**.

Non-independent research must:

■   Be clearly identified as a **marketing communication**

■   Contain a clear and prominent statement that it does not follow the requirements of independent research and is not subject to prohibitions on dealing ahead of dissemination of research

Financial promotions rules apply to non-independent research as if it were a marketing communication.

Firms must take **reasonable care** to ensure that research recommendations are fairly presented, and to disclose its interests or indicate conflicts of interest.

Situations where conflicts can arise include:

■   Employees trading in financial instruments which they know the firm has or intends to publish non-independent research about, before clients have had a reasonable opportunity to act on the research (other than where the firm is acting as a market maker in good faith, or in the execution of an unsolicited client order

■   Non-independent research intended first for internal use and for later publication to clients

7.3.4 Research recommendations: required disclosures

The **identity** (name, job title, name of firm, competent authority) of the person responsible for the research should be disclosed clearly and prominently.

The research should meet certain **general standards** for example to ensure that facts are distinguished from interpretations or opinions. Projections should be labelled as such. Reliable sources should be used, and any doubts about reliability clearly indicated. The substance of the recommendations should be possible to be substantiated by the FSA on request.

Additionally, the firm must take reasonable care to ensure **fair presentation**, broadly covering the following aspects.

■   Indication of material sources, including the issuer (if appropriate)
■   Disclosure of whether the recommendation was disclosed to the issuer and then amended
■   Summary of valuation basis or methodology
■   Explanation of the meaning of any recommendation (e.g. 'buy', 'sell', 'hold')
■   Risk warning if appropriate
■   Planned frequency of updates
■   Date of release of research, and date and time of prices mentioned
■   Details of change over any previous recommendation in the last year

Firms must make **disclosures** in research recommendations broadly covering the following areas.

■   All **relationships and circumstances** (including those of affiliated companies) that may reasonably be expected to impair the objectivity of the recommendation (especially, financial interests in any relevant investment, and a conflict of interest regarding the issuer)

■   Whether employees involved have **remuneration** tied to investment banking transactions

■   **Shareholdings** held by the firm (or an affiliated company) of over 5% of the share capital of the issuer

- **Shareholdings** held by the issuer of over 5% of the share capital of the firm (or an affiliated company)

- Other **significant financial interests**

- Statements about the **role of the firm** as market maker, lead manager of previous offers of the issuer in the last year, provider of investment banking services

- Statements about **arrangements** to prevent and avoid conflicts of interest, prices and dates at which employees involved acquired shares

- **Data** on the proportions of the firm's **recommendations** in different categories (e. g. 'buy', 'sell', 'hold'), on a quarterly basis, with the proportions of relevant investments issued by issuers who were investment banking clients of the firm during the last year

- Identification of a **third party** who produced the research, if applicable, describing also any alteration of third party recommendations and ensuring that any summary of third party research is fair, clear and not misleading

For shorter recommendations, firms can make reference to many of the relevant disclosures, e.g. by providing a web site link.

7.4 Inducements

.earning objective   **Know** the application and purpose of the rule on prohibition of inducements and the use of dealing commission, including what benefits can be supplied/obtained under such agreements

A firm must **not** pay or accept any fee or commission, or provide or receive any non-monetary benefit, in relation to designated investment business, or an ancillary service in the case of MiFID or equivalent third country business, other than:

- Fees, commissions and non-monetary benefits paid or provided to or by the client or a person on their behalf

- Fees, commissions and non-monetary benefits paid or provided to or by a third party or a person acting on their behalf, if the firm's duty to act in the best interests of the client is not impaired, and (for MiFID and equivalent business, and where there is a personal recommendation of a packaged product, but not for 'basic advice') clear, comprehensive, accurate, understandable disclosure (except of 'reasonable non-monetary benefits', listed later) is made to the client before the service is provided (Thus, the rule on inducements does not apply to discloseable commissions.)

This rule supplements Principles 1 and 6 of the *Principles for Businesses*. It deals with the delicate area of inducements and seeks to ensure that firms do not conduct business under arrangements that may give rise to conflicts of interest.

Inducements could mean anything from gifts to entertainment to bribery. The rules provide a test to help judge whether or not something is acceptable.

Where commissions must be disclosed in relation to packaged products, the firm should not enter into:

- Volume overrides, if commission on several transactions is more than a simple multiple of the commission for one transaction

- Agreements to indemnify payment of commission which might give an additional financial benefit to the recipient if the commission becomes repayable

If the firm selling packaged products enters into an agreement under which it receives commission more than that disclosed to the client, rules on disclosure of charges and inducements are likely to have been breached.

In the case of packaged products business with retail clients, there are rules to prevent a product provider from taking a **holding of capital** in the firm or providing **credit** to a firm unless stringent terms are met, including a condition requiring the holding or credit to be on commercial terms.

In relation to the sale of **packaged products**, the following are broadly deemed to be **reasonable non-monetary benefits**.

- Gifts, hospitality and promotional competition prizes of reasonable value, given by product provider to the firm

- Assistance in promotion of a firm's packaged products

- Generic product literature which enhances service to the client, with costs borne by the recipient firm

- 'Freepost' envelopes supplied by a product provider

- Product specific literature

- Content for publication in another firm's magazine, if costs are paid at market rate

- Seminar / conference attendance by a product provider, if for a genuine business purpose, with costs paid being reasonable

- 'Freephone' links

- Quotations and projections, and advice on completion of forms

- Access to data and data processing, related to the product provider's business

- Access to third party dealing and quotation systems, related to the product provider's business

- Appropriate informational software

- Cash or other assistance to develop computer facilities and software, if cost savings are generated

- Information about sources of mortgage finance

- Generic technical information

- Training facilities

- Reasonable travel and accommodation expenses, e. g. to meetings, training and market research participation

If a product provider makes benefits available to one firm but not another, this is more likely to impair compliance with the **client's best interests rule**.

Most firms deliver against the inducements requirements by drafting detailed '**gifts policies**' (although the rule does **not** explicitly require firms to have a gifts policy). These contain internal rules regarding disclosure, limits and clearance procedures for gifts.

7.5 Use of dealing commission

The practice of **using dealing commission** (previously called **soft commission**) dates back many years. The practice developed from brokers effectively **rebating** part of the commission paid by large fund management clients, to be used to cover the costs of services such as equity research. The effect was to reduce the 'real' commission paid for the execution of the trade. It is deemed necessary to control these arrangements to ensure that customers who ultimately pay the commissions, namely the fund managers' clients, are protected from abuse.

The rules on the use of dealing commission aim to ensure that an investment manager's arrangements, in relation to dealing commissions spent on acquiring services in addition to execution, are transparent and demonstrate accountability to customers so that customers are treated fairly.

The rules therefore help to ensure firms comply with Principle 1 (Integrity), Principle 6 (Customers' Interests) and Principle 8 (Conflicts of Interest).

The rules on the use of dealing commission apply to investment managers when executing customer orders through a broker or another person in shares or other investments which relate to shares, e.g. warrants, hybrids (ADRs and options) and rights to, or interests in, investments relating to shares.

When the investment manager passes on the broker's or other person's charges (whether commission or otherwise) to its customers and in return arranges to receive goods or services **the rules require the investment manager to be satisfied that the goods or services:**

- Relate to the execution of trades, or
- Comprise the provision of research

This is subject to a clause that the goods or services will reasonably assist the investment manager in the provision of services to its customers and do not impair compliance with the duty of the investment manager to act in the best interests of its customers.

In relation to **goods or services** relating to the execution of trades, the FSA have confirmed that post-trade analytics, e.g. performance measurement, is not going to be an acceptable use of dealing commission. Where the goods or services relate to research, the investment manager will have to be satisfied that the research:

- Is capable of **adding value** to the investment or trading decisions by providing **new insights** that inform the investment manager when making such decisions about its customers' portfolios

- In whatever form its output takes, represents **original thought**, in the critical and careful consideration and assessment of new and existing facts, and does not merely repeat or repackage what has been presented before

- Has **intellectual rigour** and does not merely state what is commonplace or self-evident, and

- Involves analysis or manipulation of data to reach **meaningful conclusions**

Examples of goods or services that relate to the execution of trades or the provision of research that are **not** going to be **acceptable** to the FSA include the following.

- Services relating to the valuation or performance measurement of portfolios

- Computer hardware

- Dedicated telephone lines and other connectivity services

- Seminar fees

- Subscriptions for publications

- Travel, accommodation or entertainment costs

- Order and execution management systems

- Office administration computer software, e.g. for word processing or accounting

- Membership fees to professional associations

- Purchase or rental of standard office equipment or ancillary facilities

- Employees' salaries

- Direct money payments

- Publicly available information

- Custody services relating to designated investments belonging to, or managed for, customers other than those services that are incidental to the execution of trades

Investment managers must make **adequate prior disclosure** to customers about receipt of goods and services that relate to the execution of trades or the provision of research. This should form part of the summary form disclosure under the rule on inducements. **Periodic disclosures** made on an annual basis are recommended.

7.6 Best execution

Understand the requirements of providing best execution

The basic COBS rule of **best execution** is as follows.

A firm must take all reasonable steps to obtain, when executing orders, the best possible result for its clients taking into account the execution factors.

When a firm is **dealing on own account with clients**, this is considered to be execution of client orders, and is therefore subject to the best execution rule.

If a firm provides a best quote to a client, it is acceptable for the quote to be executed after the client accepts it, provided the quote is not manifestly out of date.

The obligation to obtain best execution needs to be interpreted according to the particular type of financial instrument involved, but the rule applies to **all types of financial instrument**.

The **best execution criteria** are that the firm must take into account **characteristics of**:

- The client, including categorisation as retail or professional
- The client order
- The financial instruments
- The execution venues

The '**best possible result**' must be determined in terms of **total consideration** – taking into account any costs, including the firm's own commissions in the case of competing execution venues, and not just quoted prices. (However, the firm is not expected to compare the result with that of clients of other firms.) Commissions structure must not discriminate between execution venues.

7.7 Order execution policy

Understand the requirements for an order execution policy, its disclosure, the requirements for consent and review

Understand the rules on following specific instructions from a client

Understand the rules on monitoring the effectiveness of execution arrangements and policy; demonstrating compliance with the execution policy; and the duties of portfolio managers and receivers and transmitters to act in a client's best interest

7.7.1 Policy requirements

The firm must establish and implement an **order execution policy**, and it must monitor its effectiveness regularly.

The policy must include, for each class of financial instruments, information on different execution venues used by the firm, and the factors affecting choice of execution venue.

The firm should choose venues that enable it to obtain on a consistent basis the best possible result for execution of client orders. For each client order, the firm should apply its execution policy with a view to achieving the best possible result for the client.

If orders may be executed outside a regulated market or multilateral trading facility, this must be disclosed, and clients must give prior express consent.

A firm must be able to demonstrate to clients, on request, that it has followed its execution policy.

7.7.2 Client consent and clients' specific instructions

The firm must provide a **retail client** with details on its execution policy before providing the service, covering the relative importance the firm assigns to execution factors, a list of execution venues on which the firm relies, and a clear and prominent warning that **specific instructions** by the client could prevent the firm from following its execution policy steps fully.

If the client gives **specific instructions**, the firm has met its best execution obligation if it obtains the best result in following those instructions. The firm should not induce a client to gives such instructions, if they could prevent best execution from being obtained. However, the firm may invite the client to choose between execution venues.

The firm must obtain the **prior consent** of clients to its execution policy, and the policy must be **reviewed annually** and whenever there is a material change in the firm's ability to achieve the best possible result consistently from execution venues.

7.7.3 Portfolio management and order reception and transmission services

Firms who act as **portfolio managers** must comply with the **clients' best interests rule** when placing orders with other entities. Firms who provide a service of **receiving and transmitting orders** must do the same when transmitting orders to other entities for execution. Such firms must:

- Take all reasonable steps to obtain the best possible result for clients

- Establish and maintain a policy to enable it to do so, and monitor its effectiveness

- Provide appropriate information to clients on the policy

- Review the policy annually or whenever there is a material change affecting the firm's ability to continue to obtain the best possible result for clients

7.8 Client order handling

earning objective **Understand** the rule on client order handling and the conditions to be satisfied when carrying out client orders

The general rule on **client order handling** is that firms must implement procedures and arrangements which provide for the prompt, fair and expeditious execution of client orders, relative to other orders or the trading interests of the firm.

These procedures and arrangements must allow for the execution of otherwise comparable orders in accordance with the time of their reception by the firm.

When carrying out **client orders**, firms must:

- Ensure that orders are promptly and accurately recorded and allocated
- Carry out otherwise comparable orders sequentially and promptly, unless this is impracticable or not in clients' interests
- Inform a retail client about any material difficulty in carrying out orders promptly, on becoming aware of it

Where it is not practicable to treat orders sequentially e.g. because they are received by different media, they should not be treated as 'otherwise comparable'.

Firms must not allow the **misuse of information** relating to pending client orders. Any use of such information to deal on own account should be considered a misuse of the information.

When overseeing or arranging **settlement**, a firm must take reasonable steps to ensure that instruments or funds due are delivered to the client account promptly and correctly.

7.9 Aggregation and allocation

Learning objective

Understand the rules on aggregation and allocation of orders and the rules on aggregation and allocation of transactions for own account

Aggregation (grouping together) of client orders with other client orders or a transaction for own account is not permitted unless:

- It is unlikely to work to the disadvantage to any of the clients
- It is disclosed to each client that the effect of aggregation may work to its disadvantage
- An **order allocation policy** is established and implemented, covering the fair allocation of aggregated orders, including how the volume and price of orders determines allocations, and the treatment of partial executions

The order allocation policy must prevent reallocation of transactions on own account executed in combination with client orders, in a way that is detrimental to the client(e.g. if unfair precedence is given to the firm or another person).

If a firm aggregates a client order with a transaction on own account, and the aggregated order is partially executed, it must allocate the related trades **to the client in priority** to the firm, although if it can demonstrate that the aggregation enabled advantageous terms to be obtained, it may allocate the transaction proportionally.

7.10 Client limit orders

Learning objective

Know the rules on client limit orders – the obligation to make unexecuted client limit orders public

A **limit order** specifies a limit at or below which a client agrees to buy, or at or above which a client agrees to sell.

Unless the client expressly instructs otherwise, a firm has an obligation to make unexecuted client limit orders (for shares on a regulated market) public, to facilitate the earliest possible execution. The order may be made public by transmitting it to a regulated market or multilateral trading facility.

For **eligible counterparties**, this obligation to disclose applies only where the counterparty is explicitly sending a limit order to a firm for its execution.

The obligation to make public will not apply to a limit order that is **large** in scale compared with the **normal market size** for the share.

LEARNING MEDIA

7.11 Personal account dealing

arning objectives

Understand the application and purpose of the personal account dealing rule and the restrictions on personal account dealing

Know the arrangements required to comply with the personal account dealing rules including the notification requirements, and exceptions regarding personal account dealing

Personal account dealing relates to trades undertaken by the staff of a regulated business for themselves. Such trades can create **conflicts of interest** between staff and customers.

A firm conducting **designated investment business** must establish, implement and maintain adequate **arrangements** aimed at preventing employees who are involved in activities where a conflict of interest could occur, or who has access to inside information, from:

- Entering into a transaction which is prohibited under the **Market Abuse Directive**, or which involves misuse or improper disclosure of confidential information, or conflicts with an obligation of the firm to a customer under the regulatory system

- Except in the course of his job, advising or procuring anyone else to enter into such a transaction

- Except in the course of his job, disclosing any information or opinion to another person if the person disclosing it should know that, as a result, the other person would be likely to enter into such a transaction or advise or procure another to enter into such a transaction

The **firm's arrangements** under these provisions must be designed to ensure that:

- All relevant persons (staff involved) are aware of the personal dealing restrictions

- The firm is informed promptly of any personal transaction

- A service provider to whom activities are outsourced maintain a record of personal transactions and provides it to the firm promptly on request

- A record is kept of personal transactions notified to the firm or identified by it, including any related authorisation or prohibition

The rule on personal account dealing is **disapplied** for personal transactions:

- Under a discretionary portfolio management service where there has been no prior communication between the portfolio manager and the person for whom the transaction is executed

- In UCITS collective undertakings (e.g. OEICs and unit trusts) where the person is not involved in its management

- In life policies

- For successive personal transactions where there were prior instructions in force, nor to the termination of the instruction provided that no financial instruments are sold at the same time

7.12 Churning and switching

earning objective

Understand the guidance on churning and switching

Churning and switching are similar wrongs. They involve the cynical **overtrading** of customer accounts for the purpose of generating commission. This would clearly contravene the **client's best interests rule**.

The difference between the two lies in the **different products** in which the transactions are undertaken.

- **Churning** relates to investments generally
- **Switching** describes overtrading within and between packaged products

Churning or switching will often be difficult to isolate, unless blatant. Much would depend upon the market conditions prevailing at the time of dealing.

The **COBS rules** on churning and switching state that:

- A series of transactions that are each suitable when viewed in isolation may be unsuitable if the recommendations or the decisions to trade are made with a frequency that is not in the best interests of the client

- A firm should have regard to the client's agreed investment strategy in determining the frequency of transactions. This would include, for example, the need to switch within or between packaged products

8 REPORTING TO CLIENTS

Learning objective   **Know** the requirement to report to your client including confirmation of transactions and periodic statements

8.1 Reporting executions

In respect of **MiFID** and equivalent third country business, a firm must ensure that clients receive **adequate reports** on the services provided to it by the firm and their costs.

A firm must provide promptly in a durable medium the **essential information** on **execution of orders** to clients in the course of **designated investment business**, when it is not managing the investments. The information may be sent to an agent of the client, nominated by the client in writing.

For retail clients, a notice confirming execution must be sent as soon as possible and no later than the first business day following receipt of confirmation from the third party.

Firms must supply information about the **status of a client's order** on request.

For **series of orders** to buy units or shares in a collective undertaking (such as a **regular savings plan**), after the initial report, further reports must be provided at least at six-monthly intervals.

Where an order is executed in tranches, the firm may supply the price for each tranche or an average price. The price for each tranche must be made available on the request of a retail client.

For business that is not MiFID or equivalent third country business, confirmations need **not** be supplied if:

- The client has agreed not to receive them (with informed written consent, in the case of retail clients), or

- The designated investment is a life policy or a personal pension scheme (other than a SIPP), or

- The designated investment is held in a CTF and the information is contained in the annual statement

Copies of confirmations dispatched must be **kept** for at least **five years**, for MiFID and equivalent third country business, and for at least **three years** in other cases.

Information to be included in trade confirmations to a retail client

- Reporting firm identification
- Name / designation of client
- Trading day and time
- Order type (e.g. limit order / market order)
- Venue identification
- Instrument identification
- Buy / sell indicator (or nature of order, if not buy/sell)
- Quantity
- Unit price
- Total consideration
- Total commissions and expenses charged with, if requested, itemised breakdown
- Currency exchange rate, where relevant
- Client's responsibilities regarding settlement, including time limit for payment or delivery, and appropriate account details where not previously notified
- Details if the client's counterparty was in the firm's group or was another client, unless trading was anonymous

8.2 Periodic reporting

A firm **managing investments** on behalf of a client must provide a periodic statement to the client in a durable medium, unless such a statement is provided by another person. The statement may be sent to an agent nominated by the client in writing.

Information to be included in a periodic report

- Name of the firm
- Name / designation of retail client's account
- Statement of contents and valuation of portfolio, including details of:
    - Each designated investment held, its market value or, if unavailable, its fair value
    - Cash balance at beginning and end of reporting period
    - Performance of portfolio during reporting period
- Total fees and charges, itemising total management fees and total execution costs
- Comparison of period performance with any agreed investment performance benchmark
- Total dividends, interest and other payments received in the period
- Information about other corporate actions giving rights to designated investments held

For a **retail client**, the **periodic statement** should be provided once every **six months**, except that:

- In the case of a leveraged portfolio, it should be provided at least **once a month**
- It should be provided every **three months** if the client requests it (The firm must inform clients of this right.)
- If the retail client elects to receive information on a transaction-by-transaction basis and there are no transactions in derivatives or similar instruments giving rise to a cash settlement, the periodic statement must be supplied at least once every **twelve months**

A firm managing investments (or operating a retail client account that includes an uncovered open position in a contingent liability transaction – involving a potential liability in excess of the cost) must report to the client any **losses** exceeding any **predetermined threshold** agreed with the client.

Periodic statements for **contingent liability transactions** may include information on the **collateral value** and **option account valuations** in respect of each option written by the client in the portfolio at the end of the relevant period.

For **non-MiFID business**, a firm need not provide a periodic statement to a client habitually resident outside the UK if the client does not wish to receive it, nor in respect of a **CTF** if the annual statement contains the periodic information.

9   CLIENT ASSETS RULES

Learning objective	**Understand** the purpose of the client money and custody rules in CASS, including the requirement for segregation and that it is held in trust

9.1 Introduction

The rules in this section link to Principle 10 of the *Principles for Businesses*. The rules aim to restrict the commingling of client's and firm's assets and minimise the risk of client's investments being used by the firm without the client's agreement or contrary to the client's wishes, or being treated as the firm's assets in the event of its **insolvency**. The focus therefore is on two main issues, namely custody of investments, and client money.

The client assets rules have a broader coverage than the rules contained in COBS, the Conduct of Business Sourcebook, in that they afford protection not only to retail and professional clients, but also to **eligible counterparties**.

As we have seen earlier in this Study Book, under MiFID, client assets are regulated by the **home state**. Therefore, for example, if a French firm is **passporting** into the UK, it will adhere to French client assets rules.

The implementation of MiFID has resulted in more onerous requirements on firms in respect of custody of client assets and client money.

- Except in the case of credit institutions, firms may not use client funds for their own account in any circumstances.

- Sub-custodians and depositaries must be selected in accordance with specified rules.

- There are rules specifying that client funds be held with particular types of bank and (if the client does not object) certain money market funds meeting specified criteria.

- One of the most significant impacts of MiFID implementation on the existing client money regime is that MiFID firms will no longer be able to allow professional clients to 'opt-out' of the client money rules, for MiFID business.

The **Client Assets (CASS)** section of the FSA Handbook includes custody rules for **custody** and **client money** which apply to a firm which holds financial instruments belonging to a client in the course of the firm's **MiFID business**.

Separate '**Non-directive custody rules**' in CASS apply to other firms which receive money from clients, or hold money for them, in the course of **designated investment business** other than MiFID business. Firms subject to the non-directive custody rules may opt in to the MiFID custody rules if they elect (and keep a written record of the election) to do so. Under the non-directive custody rules for designated investment business, 'opt out' rules allow a firm to enable a professional client or an eligible counterparty to choose whether their money is subject to the client money rules. However, there is no such 'opt out' in respect of MiFID business, as noted above.

You are expected to have knowledge of the **custody and client money rules for MiFID business** and these rules are covered below.

9.2 Holding client assets

Firms sometimes hold investments on behalf of clients in physical form, e.g. bearer bonds, or may be responsible for the assets but not physically holding them as they are held elsewhere, e.g. with another custodian or via CREST.

Firms which hold financial instruments belonging to clients must make arrangements to **safeguard clients' ownership rights**, especially in the event of the firm's insolvency. Firms are not permitted to use financial instruments which are held for clients **for their own account** unless they have the express consent of the client.

The firm must have **adequate organisational arrangements** to minimise risk of loss or diminution of clients' financial instruments or of rights over them resulting from misuse, fraud, poor administration, inadequate record-keeping or other negligence.

As far as practicable, the firm must effect registration or recording of legal title to financial instruments, normally in the name of:

- The client, or
- A nominee company

For nominee companies controlled by the firm, the firm has the same level of responsibility to the client regarding custody of the assets.

In the case of **overseas financial instruments**, where it is in the client's best interests, the instruments may be held by:

- Any other party, in which case the client must be notified in writing

- The firm, subject to written consent (if a retail client) or notification of the client (for professional clients)

9.3 Requirement to protect client money

A firm must make adequate arrangements to safeguard clients' rights over **client money** the firm holds, and to prevent the use of client money for the firm's own account.

As with financial instruments, the firm must have **adequate organisational arrangements** to minimise risk of loss or diminution of clients' money or of rights over such money resulting from misuse, fraud, poor administration, inadequate record-keeping or other negligence.

If a firm leaves some of its own money in a client money account, this will be referred to as a '**pollution of trust**' and, if the firm fails, the liquidator will be able to seize all the money held in the client account for the general creditors of the firm.

9.4 Client bank accounts

Client money must be deposited with:

- A central bank
- An EEA credit institution
- A bank authorised in a third country, or
- A qualifying money market fund

Learning objective **Know** the requirements for reconciling client assets and client money including the timing and identification of discrepancies

9.5 Financial instruments: reconciliations with external records

The firm should ensure that any **third party** holding clients' **financial instruments** provides regular statements.

To ensure accuracy of its records, the firm must carry out regular reconciliations between its own records and those of such third parties:

- As regularly as is necessary, and
- As soon as possible after the date to which the reconciliation relates

The person, who may be an employee of the firm, carrying out the reconciliation should, whenever possible, be someone who is independent of the process of producing and maintaining the records. (This type of control is called **segregation of duties**.)

If a firm has not complied with the reconciliation requirements 'in any material respect', then it must inform the FSA without delay.

9.6 Financial instruments: reconciliation discrepancies

Any **discrepancies** revealed in the reconciliations – including items recorded in a suspense or error account – must be corrected promptly.

Any unreconciled shortfall must be made good, if there are reasonable grounds for concluding that the firm is responsible. If the firm concludes that someone else is responsible, steps should be taken to resolve the position with that other person.

If a firm has not made good an unreconciled shortfall 'in any material respect', then it must inform the FSA without delay.

9.7 Client money: reconciliations with external records

Broadly, if a firm holds money that belongs to someone else, then that money is client money.

As with financial instruments, to ensure accuracy of its records, the firm must carry out regular reconciliations between its own client money records and those of third parties, such as a bank, holding **client money**:

- As regularly as is necessary, and
- As soon as possible after the date to which the reconciliation relates

In determining the **frequency** of reconciliations, the firm should **consider relevant risks**, such as the nature, volume and complexity of the business, and where the client money is held.

The FSA recommends that reconciliations should compare and identify discrepancies between:

- The balance of each **client bank account** as recorded by the firm, *and* the balance shown on the bank's statement, and

- The balance as shown in the firm's records, currency by currency, on each **client transaction account** – for **contingent liability investments**, which includes certain derivatives, spot forex trades, spread bets and contracts for difference (CFDs) – *and* the balance shown in the third party's records.

Any **approved collateral** held must be included in the reconciliation.

9.8 Client money: reconciliation discrepancies

The **reason** for any **discrepancy** must be identified, unless it arises solely from timing differences between a third party's accounting systems and those of the firm.

Any **shortfall** must be paid into (or any **excess** withdrawn from) the client bank account by the close of business on the day the reconciliation is performed.

If a firm cannot resolve a difference between its internal records and those of a third party holding client money, the firm must pay its own money into a relevant account to make up any difference, until the matter is resolved.

As with financial instruments held, If a firm has not complied with the reconciliation requirements in respect of client money 'in any material respect', then it must inform the FSA without delay.

9.9 Statutory trust

Section 139(1) FSMA 2000 provides for creation of a fiduciary relationship (a **statutory trust**) between the firm and its client, under which client money is in the legal ownership of the firm but remains in the beneficial ownership of the client.

In the event of failure of the firm, costs relating to the distribution of client money may have to be borne by the trust.

Learning objective **Know** the exemptions from the requirements of the CASS rules

9.10 Exemptions from CASS rules

There are some circumstances in which the client money rules do not apply.

9.10.1 Credit institutions

The client money rules do not apply to **Banking Consolidation Directive (BCD) credit institutions** in respect of deposits. Institutions whose business is to receive deposits from the public are credit institutions.

9.10.2 Coins held for intrinsic value

Client money rules do not apply to **coins** held on behalf of a client, if the firm and client have agreed that the money is to be held by the firm for the **intrinsic value** of the **metal** in the coin.

9.10.3 DVP transactions

Money arising through **delivery versus payment (DVP) transactions** through a commercial settlement system need not be treated as client money, if it is intended that:

- Money from the client, in respect of a client's purchase, will be due to the firm within one business day, on fulfilment of a delivery obligation, or

- Money is due to the client, in respect of a client's sale, within one business day following the client's fulfilment of a delivery obligation

DVP is a form of securities trading in which payment and transfer of the subject security occur simultaneously.

9.10.4 Discharge of fiduciary duty

Money **ceases to be client money** if it is paid:

- To the client or his authorised representative

- Into a bank account of the client

- To the firm itself, when it is due and payable to the firm, or is an excess in the client bank account

- To a third party, on the client's instruction, unless it is transferred to a third party to effect a transaction – for example, a payment to an intermediate broker as initial or variation margin on behalf of a client who has a position in derivatives. In these circumstances, the firm remains responsible for that client's equity balance held at the intermediate broker until the contract is terminated and all of that client's positions at that broker closed

CHAPTER ROUNDUP

- The Conduct of Business Sourcebook (COBS) generally applies to authorised firms engaged in designated investment business carried out from their (or their appointed representatives') UK establishments. Some COB rules do not apply to eligible counterparty business.

- "Designated investment business' is business involving regulated activities, except mortgages, deposits, pure protection policies, general insurance, Lloyd's business and funeral plans.

- The level of protection given to clients by the regulatory system depends on their classification, with retail clients being protected the most. Professional clients and eligible counterparties may both be either *per se* or elective. Both professional clients and eligible counterparties can re-categorise to get more protection.

- Firms doing designated investment business, except advising, must set out a basic client agreement. Firms must provide to clients appropriate information about the firm and its services, designated investments and their risks, execution venues and costs. Firms managing investments must establish a performance benchmark and must provide information about valuations and management objectives.

- There are special disclosure rules where a personal recommendation to buy a packaged product is given to a retail client: the IDD and 'menu' will be provided to the client.

- It is generally acceptable for a firm to rely on information provided by others if the other firm is competent and not connected with the firm placing the reliance.

- A financial promotion inviting someone to engage in investment activity must be issued by or approved by an authorised firm. Communications must be fair, clear and not misleading. Prospectus advertisements must clearly indicate that they are not a prospectus. Communications with retail clients must balance information about benefits of investments with information about risks.

- Unwritten financial promotions rules cover cold calling, which must be limited to an 'appropriate time of day'.

- Rules on assessing suitability of the recommendation apply when a firm makes a personal recommendation in relation to a designated investment.

- For certain packaged products, a suitability report is required, specifying the client's demands and needs and explaining the firm's recommendation.

- There are obligations to assess 'appropriateness' – based on information about the client's experience and knowledge – for MiFID business other than making a personal recommendation and managing investments.

- Key Features Documents, which must be produced to at least the same quality as marketing material, disclose product information for packaged products.

- Retail clients must be given the opportunity to change their mind (cancel) after agreeing to the purchase of a packaged product.

- Firms must seek to ensure fair treatment if there could be a conflict of interest. Common platform firms must maintain an effective conflicts of interest policy. Conflicts of interest policies must cover financial analysts producing investment research.

- Inducements must not be given if they conflict with acting in the best interests of clients, and there are controls on the use of dealing commission.

- A firm must in general take all reasonable steps to obtain, when executing orders, the best possible result for its clients. This is the requirement of best execution. There must be arrangements for prompt, fair and expeditious client order handling, and a fair order allocation policy. Unexecuted client limit orders must normally be made public, to facilitate early execution.

- Firms must establish arrangements designed to prevent employees entering into personal transactions which are prohibited forms of market abuse. Staff must be made aware of the personal dealing restrictions.

- Churning (investments generally) and switching (packaged products) forms of unsuitable overtrading of customer accounts in order to generate commission.

- There are requirements to send out confirmation notes promptly, and periodic statements (valuations) regularly.

- Client assets rules aim to restrict the commingling of client's and firm's assets and to prevent misuse of client's investments by the firm without the client's agreement, or being treated as the firm's assets in the event of the firm's insolvency.

TEST YOUR KNOWLEDGE

Check your knowledge of the Chapter here, without referring back to the text.

1.	Name the three main categories of client.	▪ ▪ ▪
2.	Name three types of *per se* eligible counterparty.	▪ ▪ ▪
3.	List the different types of packaged product.	▪ ▪ ▪ ▪ ▪
4.	What different types of 'scope' may apply to a firm selling packaged products?	▪ ▪ ▪
5.	What is the full title of the 'menu'?	
6.	A firm's communications and financial promotions must be '....., ... and not ...'. *Fill in the blanks.*	▪ ▪ ▪
7.	What is the FPO?	
8.	What information will the firm need to obtain from the client to enable it to assess the appropriateness of a product or service to the client?	
9.	What are the main section of a Key Features Document?	▪ ▪ ▪ ▪

10.	On what grounds (i.e., stating what reasons) may a consumer cancel or withdraw from a contract?	
11.	What is the name for administrative and physical barriers and other internal arrangements, designed to contain sensitive information?	
12.	What does the rule on best execution require?	
13.	What is the difference between a Confirmation Note and a Periodic Statement?	
14.	What is the effect of a statutory trust created under section 139(1) FSMA 2000?	

Test Your Knowledge: Answers

1. Eligible counterparties, professional clients and retail clients.

   (See Section 2.2)

2. Investment firms, national governments and central banks are all examples.

   (See Section 2.2.4)

3. Use the mnemonic CLIPS: Collective Investment Schemes (regulated); Life policies; Investment trust savings schemes; Personal pensions; Stakeholder pensions.

   (See Section 3.9.1)

4. A firm's scope may be:

   - The whole of the market or market sector
   - Limited to several product providers
   - Limited to a single product provider

   (See Section 3.9.2)

5. 'Key Facts: A Guide to the Cost of Our Services'

   (See Section 3.9.5)

6. Fair, clear and not misleading.

   (See Section 4.4.)

7. The FPO is the Financial Promotions Order. It contains a number of exemptions from S21 FSMA and the FSA's rules on financial promotions.

   (See Section 4.8)

8. The firm will need to ask the client for information about his knowledge and experience in the relevant investment field, so that it can assess whether the client understands the risks involved

   (See Section 5.4)

9. After the title, 'Key features of the [name of product]', the prescribed sections are: 'Its aims'; 'Your commitment' / 'Your investment'; 'Risks'; 'Questions and Answers'.

   (See Section 6.1.3)

10. There are no specified 'grounds': the consumer need not give any reason for exercising the right to cancel.

    (See Section 6.3.4)

11. 'Chinese walls'.

    (See Section 7.2.)

12. The best execution rule requires a firm to take all reasonable steps to obtain, when executing orders, the best possible result for its clients, taking into account the execution factors.

    (See Section 7.6)

13. A Confirmation Note confirms the essential details of each trade and must be sent out within one business of the trade date (within T + 1). A periodic statement gives the value and contents of a portfolio and is normally sent out every six months.

    (See Sections 8.1 and 8.2)

14. Section 139(1) FSMA 2000 provides for creation of a fiduciary relationship (a statutory trust) between the firm and its client, under which client money is in the legal ownership of the firm but remains in the beneficial ownership of the client.

    (See Section 9.9)

6
Complaints and Redress

INTRODUCTION

An aggrieved customer may pursue an unresolved complaint against a firm with the Financial Services Ombudsman (FOS) or, ultimately, the Courts.

Before going to the FOS, the customer must first give the firm a chance to put things right. The FSA expects firms to maintain 'effective and transparent' complaints handling procedures.

The Financial Services Compensation Scheme gives limited compensation to investors when a financial services firm fails.

BPP
LEARNING MEDIA

Customer complaints

- **Know** the procedures a firm must implement and follow to handle customer complaints

- **Know** the role of the Financial Ombudsman Service (FOS) and the awards which can be awarded

- **Know** the criteria for a complainant to be eligible to lodge a complaint

- **Know** the circumstances in which the Financial Services Compensation Scheme will pay compensation and the compensation payable in respect of protected deposits and protected investment business

Exam tip

Bear in mind that, out of the 50 questions in the paper, you are likely to be asked just one or two questions on the content of this chapter.

1 CUSTOMER COMPLAINTS PROCEDURES

| **Know** the procedures a firm must implement and follow to handle customer complaints

1.1 General points

Firms carrying on regulated activities may receive **complaints** from their clients about the way the firm has provided financial services or in respect of failure to provide a financial service. This could include allegations of financial loss whether or not such losses have actually yet occurred: for example, in the case of a mis-sold pension contract, future losses may be involved. Under the FSA's rules, a firm must have **procedures** to ensure complaints from eligible complainants are properly handled.

A **complaint** is defined as 'any **oral or written** expression of dissatisfaction, whether justified or not, from, or on behalf of, a person about the provision of, or failure to provide, a financial service, which alleges that the complainant has suffered (or may suffer) financial loss, material distress or material inconvenience'.

Firms are permitted to **outsource complaints handling**, or to arrange a 'one-stop shop' for handling complaints with other firms.

1.2 Eligible complainants

The rules on how firms must handle complaints apply to **eligible complainants**. An eligible complainant is a person eligible to have a complaint considered under the Financial Ombudsman Service.

Eligible complainants comprise: private **individuals**, **businesses** with a group annual turnover of less than £1m, **charities** with an annual income of less than £1m or trusts with net asset value of less than £1m (other than those who are properly classified as **professional clients or eligible counterparties**) who are customers or potential customers of the firm.

The rules do not apply to **authorised professional firms** (such as firms of accountants or solicitors) in respect of their **non-mainstream regulated activities**.

For **MiFID business**, the **complaints handling and record rules** apply to:

- Complaints from **retail clients**, but not those who are not retail clients.

- Activities carried on from a **branch** of a UK firm in another EEA state, but not to activities carried on from a branch of an EEA firm in the UK.

- If a firm takes responsibility for activities **outsourced** to a third party processor, the firm is responsible for dealing with complaints about those activities.

1.3 Consumer awareness rule

To aid **consumer awareness** of the complaints protection offered, firms must:

- Publish a **summary** of their internal processes for dealing with complaints promptly and fairly.
- Refer eligible customers in writing to this summary at, or immediately after, the point of sale.
- Provide the summary on request, or when acknowledging a complaint.

1.4 Complaints handling

Firms, and UK firms' branches in the EEA, must establish procedures for the reasonable handling of complaints which:

- Are effective and transparent.

- Allow complaints to be made by any reasonable means (which might include email messages, or telephone calls, for example).

- Recognise complaints as requiring resolution.

In respect of non-MiFID business, firms must ensure that they identify any **recurring or systemic problems** revealed by complaints. For MiFID business, the requirement is that firms must use complaints information to detect and minimise risk of '**compliance failures**'.

Having regard to FSA **Principle 6** (*Customers' interests*), firms should consider acting on its own initiative in respect of customers who may have been disadvantaged but have not complained. (This is a good example of how, in line with its move towards 'principles-based regulation, the FSA expects firms to consider themselves how to apply the Principles for Businesses.)

1.5 Complaints resolution

For all complaints received, the firm must:

- Investigate the complaint **competently, diligently and impartially**

- Assess **fairly, consistently and promptly**:
  - whether the complaint should be upheld
  - what remedial action and/or redress may be appropriate
  - whether another respondent may be responsible for the matter (in which case, by the **complaints forwarding rule**, the complaint may be **forwarded** to that other firm, promptly and with notification of the reasons to the client)

- Offer any redress or remedial action

- Explain the firm's assessment of the complaint to the client, its decision, including any offer of redress or remedial action made – in a fair, clear and not misleading way

Factors relevant to assessing a complaint

- All the available evidence and circumstances
- Similarities with other complaints
- Guidance from the FSA, FOS or other regulators

The firm should aim to resolve complaints as early as possible, minimising the number of unresolved complaints referred to the FOS – with whom the firm must cooperate fully, complying promptly with any settlements or awards.

1.6 Complaints resolved the next day

Complaints **time limit, forwarding and reporting rules** do not apply to complaints which are **resolved by the next business day** after the complaint is made.

1.7 Time limit rules

On receiving a complaint, the firm must:

- Send to the complainant a prompt written acknowledgement providing 'early reassurance' that it has received the complaint and is dealing with it, and

- Ensure the complainant in kept informed of progress on the complaint's resolution thereafter.

By the end of **eight weeks** after receiving a complaint which remains unresolved, the firm must send:

- A final response, or

- A holding response, which explains why a final response cannot be made and gives the expected time it will be provided, informs the complainant of his right to complain directly to the FOS if he is not satisfied with the delay, and encloses a copy of the FOS explanatory leaflet

The FSA expects that, within eight weeks of their receipt, almost all complaints will have been substantively addressed.

1.8 Firms with a two-stage complaints procedure

Some firms operate a **two-stage complaints procedure** that provides for a complainant who is not satisfied with the firm's initial response to refer the matter back to the firm or to its head office.

These firms are subject to the time limits set out above, but the rules recognise that some complainants may never respond to the initial reply or may take a long time to do so. Therefore, where the firm sends a response to the complainant offering redress or explaining why they do not propose to give redress and setting out how the complainant can pursue the claim further within the firm or apply to the FOS, it is permissible for the firm to regard the matter as closed if the firm does not get a reply within eight weeks.

If the complainant does reply indicating that they remain dissatisfied, then the general time limits will resume. However, the firm can discount any time in excess of a week taken by the complainant to reply.

1.9 Time barring

Complaints received outside the FOS **time limits** (see below) may be rejected without considering their merits in a final response, but this response should state that the FOS may waive this requirement in exceptional circumstances.

1.10 Complaints record rule

Records of complaints and of the measures taken for their resolution must be retained for:

- **Five years**, for MiFID business
- **Three years**, for other complaints

after the date the complaint was received.

1.11 Complaints reporting

Firms must provide a complete **report to the FSA** on complaints received **twice a year**. There is a standard format for the report, which must show, for the reporting period:

- Complaints broken down into categories and generic product types

- Numbers of complaints closed by the firm: within four weeks of receipt; within four to eight weeks; and more than eight weeks from receipt

- Numbers of complaints: upheld; known to have been referred to and accepted by the FOS; outstanding at the beginning of reporting period; outstanding at the end of the reporting period

- Total amount of redress paid in respect of complaints

2 THE FINANCIAL OMBUDSMAN SERVICE

Learning objectives
Know the role of the Financial Ombudsman Service (FOS) and the awards which can be granted
Know the criteria for a complainant to be eligible to lodge a complaint

2.1 Function of the Ombudsman

A **complainant** must first go to the authorised firm against which the complaint is being made. If the authorised firm does not resolve the complaint to his satisfaction, the complainant may refer it to the **Financial Ombudsman Service (FOS)**.

The FOS offers an informal method of independent adjudication of disputes between a firm and its customer, which is relatively cheap compared with the alternative of taking action through the Courts.

2.2 Powers of the FOS

The FOS is a body set up by statute and, while its Board is appointed by the FSA, it is **independent** from the FSA and authorised firms. The FOS is, however, accountable to the FSA and is required to make an annual report to the FSA on its activities.

The FOS can consider a complaint against an authorised firm for an act or omission in carrying out any of the firm's regulated activities together with any ancillary activities that firm does. This is known as the **Compulsory Jurisdiction** of the FOS.

In addition to the Compulsory Jurisdiction, the FOS can consider a complaint under its '**Voluntary Jurisdiction**'. Firms or businesses can choose to submit to the voluntary jurisdiction of the FOS by entering into a contract with the FOS. This is available, for example, to unauthorised firms, and can cover activities such as credit and debit card transactions and ancillary activities carried on by that voluntary participant where they are not regulated activities.

A further **Consumer Credit Jurisdiction** applies under the Consumer Credit Act 2006, which gives to the FOS powers to resolve certain disputes regarding loans against holders of licences issued by the Office of Fair Trading under the Consumer Credit Act 1974.

2.3 Eligible complainants

Only **eligible complainants** who have been customers of authorised firms or of firms which have voluntarily agreed to abide by the FOS rules may use the FOS. The scope of what is meant by 'eligible complainants' is explained in section 1 of this chapter.

Where an eligible complainant refers a matter to the Ombudsman, a firm has no definitive right to block the matter being referred, but may dispute the eligibility of the complaint or the complainant. In such circumstances, the Ombudsman will seek representations from the parties. The Ombudsman may investigate the merits of the case and may also convene a hearing if necessary.

2.4 Outcome of FOS findings

Where the Ombudsman finds in favour of the complainant, it can force the firm to take appropriate steps to remedy the position including to pay up to **£100,000** plus reasonable costs (although awards of costs are not common). This figure will normally represent the financial loss the eligible complainant has suffered but can also cover any pain and suffering, damage to their reputation and any distress or inconvenience caused. If the Ombudsman considers that a sum greater than £100,000 would be fair, he can recommend that the firm pays the balance, although he cannot force the firm to pay this excess.

Once the Ombudsman has given a decision, the complainant may decide whether to accept or reject that decision.

- If the complainant **accepts** the Ombudsman's decision, **the authorised firm is bound** by it
- If the complainant **rejects** the decision, they can pursue the matter further through the **Courts**

3 COMPENSATION

Know the circumstances in which the Financial Services Compensation Scheme will pay compensation and the compensation payable in respect of protected deposits and protected investment business

3.1 Purpose of FSCS

The **Financial Services Compensation Scheme (FSCS)** is set up under FSMA 2000. The FSCS is designed to compensate **eligible claimants** where a relevant firm is unable or likely to be unable to meet claims against it. Generally speaking, therefore, the scheme will only apply where the firm is declared **insolvent or bankrupt**. The FSCS is seen as part of the 'toolkit' the FSA will use to meet its statutory objectives.

The compensation scheme is independent, but accountable, to the FSA and HM Treasury for its operations and works in partnership with the FSA in delivering the FSA's objectives, particularly that of consumer protection. The FSCS is funded by **levies on authorised firms**.

3.2 Entitlement to compensation

To be entitled to compensation from the scheme, a person must:

1   Be an **eligible claimant**. This would generally cover most individuals and small businesses. Specifically, an eligible claimant is defined as a claimant who is **not**:

 - An individual with a connection to the insolvent firm, e.g. directors

 - A large company or large partnership/mutual association. What is meant by a large company and partnership will depend on rules established under the UK Companies Acts, which are amended from time to time

 - An authorised firm, unless they are a sole trader/small business and the claim arises out of a regulated activity of which they have no experience, i.e. do not have permission to carry out

 - An overseas financial services institution, supranational body, government and local authority

2   Have a '**protected claim**'. This means certain types of claims in respect of deposits and investment business. Protected investment business means **designated investment business**, the activities of the manager/trustee of an authorised unit trust and the activities of the authorised corporate director/depository of an ICVC. These activities must be carried on either from an establishment in the UK or in an EEA state by a UK firm who is passporting their services there.

3   Be claiming against a '**relevant person**' who is **in default**. A relevant person means:

–   An authorised firm, except an EEA firm passporting into the UK (customers who lose money as a result of default by an EEA firm must normally seek compensation from the firm's home state system, unless the firm has **top-up cover** provided by the FSCS in addition to, or in the absence of, compensation provided by the home state).

–   An appointed representative of the above

4   Make the claim within the relevant **time limits** (normally six years from when the claim arose)

The scheme will normally award financial compensation in cash. The FSCS may require the eligible claimant to assign any legal rights to them in order to receive compensation as they see fit.

3.3 Compensation limits

The maximum compensation levels per claim, which has been at these levels for some time, are summarised in the Table below.

	Limit
Protected investments	£48,000 (100% of the first £30,000 and 90% of the next £20,000)
Protected deposits	£31,700 (100% of the first £2,000 and 90% of the next £33,000)

Note that the limits are per claim, and not per account or contract held.

- A claimant who has, for example, a claim against a relevant person for a deposit of £2,000, and for a further deposit of £1,500, will not receive 100% compensation on both deposits; instead he will receive £3,350 (100% of the first £2,000 and 90% of the next £1,500).

- If a claimant receives more than one payment in respect of a claim or claims on one or more protected contract of insurance, the claimant will only receive 100% of the first £2,000 of the total paid, and not 100% of the first £2,000 of each payment.

CHAPTER ROUNDUP

- Firms must have transparent and effective complaints procedures, and must make customers aware of them.

- Firms must investigate complaints competently, diligently and impartially.

- Time limits apply to complaints processing, and the firm must report data on complaints to the FSA twice-yearly.

- If the firm does not resolve a customer's complaint to the customer's satisfaction, the Financial Ombudsman Service is available to adjudicate the dispute.

- The FOS has a Compulsory Jurisdiction (covering authorised firms' regulated activities) and a Voluntary Jurisdiction (for unregulated activities where a firm opts for it).

- The FOS can order a firm to pay up to £100,000, plus costs, in respect of a complaint.

- The Financial Services Compensation Scheme – set up under FSMA 2000 to help meet the FSA's statutory objectives – will pay out within the claim limits to eligible depositors and investors if a firm becomes insolvent.

TEST YOUR KNOWLEDGE

Check your knowledge of the chapter here, without referring back to the text.

1.	What does Principle for Businesses 6 imply that firms should do in respect of customers who may have been disadvantaged but have not complained?	
2.	How quickly must a firm acknowledge a complaint?	
3.	For how long must records of complaints be kept by a firm?	■ ■
4.	What is the maximum award that the Financial Ombudsman Service can give?	■ ■
5.	What is the maximum payout for an eligible claimant under the Financial Services Compensation Scheme who had invested in stocks and shares?	■ ■
6.	A saver has two deposit accounts with a bank which fails. The balances are £2,000 and £10,000 respectively. How much compensation will be available from the FSCS?	■ ■

TEST YOUR KNOWLEDGE: ANSWERS

1. The FSA considers that it implies that firms should act on their own initiative in respect of the positions of such customers.

   (See Section 1.4)

2. The firm must send to the complainant a prompt written acknowledgement, but no time limit is specified in the rules.

   (See Section 1.7)

3. Five years, for MiFID business; three years, for other complaints, after the date the complaint was received.

   (See Section 1.10)

4. £100,000 plus costs.

   (See Section 2.4)

5. £48,000 (100% of the first £30,000 *plus* 90% of the next £20,000).

   (See Section 3.3)

6. £11,000 (100% of the first £2,000 *plus* 90% of the next £10,000).

   (See Section 3.3)

INDEX